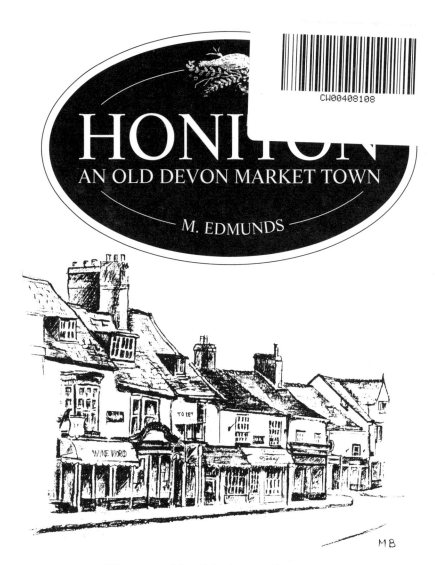

HONITON
AN OLD DEVON MARKET TOWN

M. EDMUNDS

Illustrated by Marianne Barton
Photographs by Adrian Wakley

WESTCOUNTRY
BOOKS

First published in 1993 by Westcountry Books

Copyright ⓒ M. Edmunds 1993

British Library Cataloguing-in-Publication Data

CIP Catalogue Record for this book is available
from the British Library

WESTCOUNTRY BOOKS
Publishing and Book Distribution
1 Chinon Court
Lower Moor Way
Tiverton
Devon EX16 6SS
Tel: 0884 243242
Fax: 0884 243325

ISBN 1 898 386 01 3

The cover illustration is taken from a watercolour by an unknown artist painted at sometime between 1837 and 1860. It shows the top of New Street at its junction with Marlpits Lane. (Courtesy Allhallows Museum).

ACKNOWLEDGEMENTS

Grateful acknowledgements to The Devon Record Office, The Westcountry Studies Library, Honiton Library, and Honiton Allhallows Museum for their assistance and permission to use documents and pictures. Thanks also to Lord Courtenay and the Courtenay Estate for permission to reproduce family documents; to Derek Yates, retired head of Honiton Community College, for his interest in translating Falco de Breaute's epitaph.

INTRODUCTION

Every town is, in a sense, its own history, lying in its web of old associations, buildings, streets, people. Professor W.G. Hoskins, in his *Fieldwork in Local History* says 'we live in a country that is richer than any other in the visible remains of its past.' Devon is perhaps richer in these than many other counties in England, due in part to its early isolation and to the fact that it was by-passed by the effects of the industrial revolution and the changes they brought to the face of the land. Thus today many Devon towns and villages have survived almost unchanged over the centuries.

Honiton can be said to be one of these. It has been improved, modernised, extended, but it is basically unaltered from the original borough. Its recorded history began with Domesday, but one has, from this very record, to assume that it already existed long before the great survey began. And it is to the 'visible remains' that one has to turn in order to try and piece together a background pattern of those very early years.

You can stand today in the same street where the fair was held nearly a thousand years ago and all its history will pass you by. No wars have ravaged it, for Honiton has had since early times a commendably pragmatic attitude to warring factions.

In fact it would seem to have been a town where nothing more disturbing than 'friendly' occupation disturbed its everyday life. In the eighteenth century it became one of the few boroughs in the country with a potwaller franchise and the result was almost a century of lively corruption, political invasion and endemic immorality which only ended with the Reform Laws.

Honiton went through a very bad patch in the middle of the nineteenth century mainly due to the simultaneous failure of the wool, lace and coaching industries. Richard Farquharson, local historian of the time, recorded that 'the grass grows green on the roads once beaten bare by the horses' hoofs ...'

But out of this has come the pleasant, lively little town of today, thriving on some local industries and farming but to a large extent on the growing tourist trade. For these visitors, and perhaps the residents, it may be interesting to link up this present picture with what has gone before. Not in the form of a definitive history - rather as a chronicle of past events against the fabric of Honiton today.

Honiton today from the south-east

1

The whole South West area was very sparsely populated in Palaeolithic times, and few traces of these shadowy ancestors exist in Devon. While evidence of Neolithic man has been found, it has been largely overlaid by their successors in the Bronze and Iron Ages. It is to these last and in particular the Dumnonii, 'the people of the land', from whom the name Devon evolved, that we can best identify today.

They were a Celtic, part Iberian, race who migrated here from the northern coast of France around B.C. 500. Historically regarded as farmers they were also a sea-faring people and, in the days when the Channel was more of a link than a barrier, they and the maritime Veneti of the Loire valley existed almost as one nation.

It was the Dumnonii who built most of the Iron Age forts in Devon, many of which still exist, hardly altered apart from the erosion of time. The majority in East Devon are in the narrow corridor bounded north and south by moors and sea and extending roughly between the Axe and the Exe. It is an area Hoskins would describe as 'saturated with the material evidence of the past'. Almost every road began life as an ancient trackway with alongside them the forts and the worn humps of prehistoric barrows.

The largest and probably the oldest of these earthworks, Hembury, lies to the north of present day Honiton on the Cullompton road. There is evidence here of Neolithic occupation. The Dumnonii abandoned it around A.D. 70 and the Romans are believed to have used it as a garrison for some time before Exeter became their central base. There is no doubt that it was a focal point of most traffic and trading in the area.

The greater part of Devon at this time was thickly wooded, apart from the high moors, and the Dumnonii therefore became largely hunters and herdsmen and as time passed they developed creative skills in making farm and domestic implements and utensils of increasingly high quality craftsmanship. Trade with neighbours grew and communications with the rest of the country and with the Continent improved. One result of this was that the primitive trackways gradually became more defined. The most important of these feeding the West was that from London which roughly linked settlements at Sarum (Salisbury), Dorchester and Axminster with Hembury.

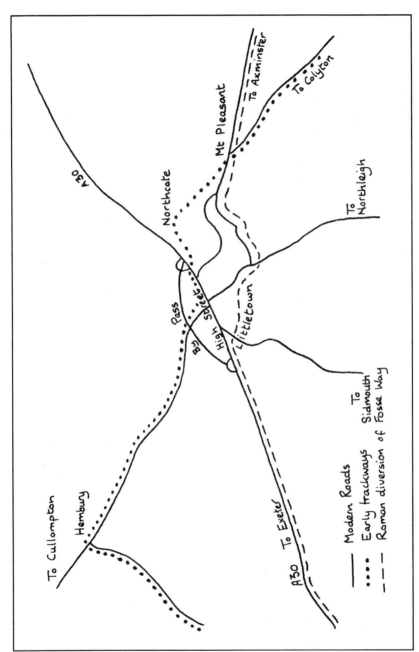

Sketch map illustrating likely routes in Roman times

The Romans certainly made good use of these old trackways when they extended their road system through Devon around the middle of the first century. The earliest followed the route referred to and, according to Ivan Margery in his *Roman Roadways in Britain*, can be traced through Wilmington to Honiton Hill 'where an ancient ridgeway from Colyton crosses diagonally from south-west to north-west and descends the escarpment directly as Northcote Lane'. Traces of this route can be found today, joining up with what is now Northcote Road and, on the far side of the new entrance to the A30, re-emerging as the truncated end of the road called Roman Way (certainly no proof of its origin, but possibly indicative of ancient association). From here it is possible to trace this road through the town to the point where, turning north, it reappears as Northcote Lane to proceed in a north-westerly direction out to Hembury.

This, however, does not seem to have been the main Roman route which later appears to have run on a parallel course south of where the town is today. This was most likely part of the re-routing of the Fosse Way which, until about A.D. 50 ran from Lincoln and terminated at the then considerable harbour at Axmouth.

The growth of Exeter as an administrative and military centre around this period resulted in a diversion of this road away from Axmouth at the point where the Fosse Way crossed the eastern route described above, somewhere around Axminster. From here it followed the existing road westward and, although evidence of a considerable highway has been found up to Mount Pleasant, there it seems to have parted company with the old route. It might be reasonable to suppose that this earlier road going to Hembury was far too circuitous to transport troops and supplies to Exeter, and that the Romans followed the parish boundary line past where Bishop Coplestone's Tower stands today. This came out above St Michael's Church, down the hill past the church, on through the settlement of Littletown, out along the present route of the Exeter Road to where the Hembury road came south via Colestocks to Straitway Head.

The coming of the Romans does not appear to have had a great deal of effect on the Dumnonii. Apart from a few skirmishes they apparently put up little effective resistance. The Romans for their part tended to leave them more or less to their own devices provided they observed the administrative laws. It was the introduction of this new law and order, together with a desire for a more expansive existence, that began to entice the Iron Age fort dwellers out of their hill-top fastnesses. In his *Britannia* William Camden says that 'Roman roads were made on almost all the world over by the Romans for the convenience of travelling and to employ the common people (that they might not grow factious by too much ease ...),''suggesting that the 'people of the land' were less likely to cause mischief if they were kept busy.

He goes on and near upon these roads were cities built, as also inns or mansions for accommodation of travellers that all the necessaries and mutations (for so these places were then called) where travellers could change their post-horses, draught beasts or wagons'.

So we have farming communities, and along with them wayside accommodation, so that even before the Saxons arrived there was a certain amount of valley settlement.

There were settlements of varying degrees of importance all along the Fosse Way, with intermediate smaller stations. Just where the missing Roman settlement of Moridunum was located has long been a mystery. There have been various theories that it was Seaton, or Hembury, but the road distances siting it in the Antonine Itinerary - 36 miles from Dorchester and 15 from Exeter - would make the Honiton area, situated as it was on such an important highway, one of the most likely places.

Honiton was certainly well placed to have been a travellers' stopping place between Axminster and Exeter, although at that period the settlement would have been at what is now Littletown centred around the manor detailed in Domesday.

With the departure of the Romans around A.D. 410, the Dumnonii again carried on much as before. Even the coming of the Saxons in the eighth century did little to disturb their lives, although many of them chose this time to return to the place of their roots, the north of France, taking with them the name of Brittany which Julius Caesar had bestowed on these islands. Those remaining lived in a sort of passive co-existence with their new conquerors. There is a mention of a battle at Bindon, near Axminster, with over 2000 Celts slain, but from this time on the people of the land tended to merge, Celt and Saxon, into one race.

William of Malmesbury records that they inhabited Exeter unilaterally to begin with, living under their separate laws, until the Wessex king Athelstan unified the whole region under his rule, introducing land organisation, the inauguration of the Hundreds for administrative purposes, and a form of ecclesiastical structure.

Devon suffered rather more from the Viking raids. In the beginning of the eleventh century these Northern raiders besieged Exeter and overran the surrounding countryside, burning and pillaging villages, no doubt including Honiton, and in 1003 ransacking the city completely; after which they moved farther afield and the county was left in peace for a while.

At the time of the Norman Conquest Devon was fairly well settled, with the hedged and enclosed landscape much as we know it today, and with many of the farms and villages dating back to pre-Saxon times. Boroughs or 'burhs' had existed since the eighth century, when they took the form of strongholds against the invading Danes. With more peaceful times they became trading posts with special privileges and later self-governing units, although still under the general control of the county sheriffs and the earls.

So that although Honiton was officially confirmed as a borough in 1300 it is described as such a hundred years earlier and was doubtless in existence long prior to this. The term 'manor' which figures so largely in Domesday was a unit of agrarian organisation common through medieval Europe and popularised in this country by the Normans.

By the time of the invasion the whole region was sufficiently well settled to put up, along with the northern parts of the country, a united front against the Norman conquerors. Exeter was the rallying point and so troublesome did the region become that, in 1068, William was obliged to lay siege to the city for eighteen days.

There is an alleged incident at this time that speaks volumes for the attitude of the rebellious Devonians. An unknown Exeter man 'having bared himself, standing on the wall, disturbed the ears with a sound from his lower parts ...'. William seems to have decided to be tolerant with such barbarians and waited until they thought fit to let him into their city and to swear loyalty. Nor did he exact any penalties for their resistance.

Scarcely a year later the sons of the defeated King Harold chose Devon for several landings to try and raise an army against William, counting on local support. However, although there was some sympathy for them, they made little headway and were eventually driven off. And life in the West settled down again.

In the great property overhaul that came with peace almost all the Saxons in Devon lost their lands. The Norman conquerors called it the Great Inquisition of 1086. The Saxons called it by their own name 'Domesdaeg' - Day of Judgement. And as Domesday we know it today. Domesday was William's conquest by book-keeping. Of the thousand Devon estates recorded in it, only around a hundred and thirty remained in the hands of owners who had held them before the Conquest. Almost three-quarters of the remainder was owned by only six men, one of whom was King William's half-brother, Robert, Count of Mortmain.

Mortmain had many estates in other parts of the country, but among his Devon acquisitions was the land which had belonged to Saxon Elmer, Earl of Devon, included in which was the 'manor called Honetona.' The tenant of Honetona named in Domesday was another Saxon, Drogo or Dreus, and he apparently continued in occupancy under the new lord.

The Exchequer Book of the Domesday Survey, to give it its full title, and in particular the Exeter Book of the survey, is of fascinating interest in getting some picture of Honiton as it must have been at the time of the compilation in 1086.

It appears to have been an established community. The manor is recorded as consisting of five hides (a hide is a somewhat variable measure of around 120 acres) which, in comparison with say Okehampton, a large manor, was a very respectable size. This supported twenty-four villeins (or farming tenants) who worked three of the hides, six bordars (or cottagers) and three serfs who were likely to have been remnants of the Dumnonii. There was also fifty acres of woodland and eighteen acres of meadow, with some pasture land.

What gives the manor some importance is the presence of a mill. Mills were rare in Devon at this time despite the abundance of streams and rivers, and this can possibly be explained by the fact that water mills were still a new and expensive device to the Devonians. Among the 983 Domesday settlements in the county only 80 had mills, one of which was Honiton.

Another interesting item is the mention of 'two salt-works rendering five shillings' in the Exchequer Domesday, and in the Exeter Domesday, of 'two salt-workers who render by the year five shilings to ferm' (or rent). Salt was a very valuable commodity at this time. Roman soldiers were paid in salt - their salarium or salary. In the whole of Devon, however, only twenty-two salt pans (*salinai*) are

St Margaret's Chapel from a drawing made in 1792

St Michael's, Honiton, drawn in 1793

listed, and only six salt-workers (*salinarii*). Although the salt-pans were generally located on the coast, they are mentioned in other inland towns. There appears to be some obscurity in the definition of *salinas* and *salinarii*, but we do know that four salt-pans at Beer had belonged to the Abbot of Horton and that by 1086 these had passed, like much else, into the hands of the Count of Mortain as part of the manor of Honetona. It would seem most likely that the two Honiton salt-workers were paying their rent of five shillings on the pans at Beer.

All this confirms a community of borough status having grown up alongside the Fosse Way in the area of what is now Littletown; this name being given in the same way as other towns with early beginnings have their Oldtown, etc. as the area from whence the settlement spread. There is no trace now of the demesne or principal dwelling of the lord of the manor but there is good reason to believe it was most likely on the site of the old Livermore Farm which used to stand just below St Michael's church.

The farm took the name of Livermore from the family of that name who farmed there in the sixteenth century, but it used also to be known as Court Hall many years ago, and the field between it and the church as Court Field. Prof. Hoskins regards ancient naming as an almost invariable clue as to the location of the demesne dwelling and he points out that this often occurs in the form of 'Great' or 'Hall Farm', 'Church Farm' or 'Court Farm'. Farquharson gives us the information that in the last century he knew of the foundations of a large mansion still existing in Court Field, also that Livermore Farm itself bore evidence of having been part of a much larger structure. Unfortunately the farm had its roof ripped off by a World War II plane and, although repaired and occupied until the 1970s, it no longer qualified as a listed building and was demolished to make way for the Haydons housing estate.

Domesday was not interested in ecclesiastical buildings, but it is likely that St Michael's existed in some form at this time, either possibly as the site of a Roman place of worship or as a wayside chapel. There are early references to it as the latter in connection with the thirteenth century Mendicant Friars and also in the Courtenay family records as a family oratory belonging to the manor house. The Courtenays became lords of the manor at the beginning of the fourteenth century and it was a Courtenay Bishop who enlarged the chapel to the present church towards the end of the next century.

Prior to this it most likely consisted of a small building covering the centre of the present chancel entered by the small Norman doorway still existing in the south-east wall of the church. But its situation in regard to the road skirting it might have been very different.

We know that as late at 1838 the entrance gate stood about fifty yards closer to the church than it does today. The gates were moved in1839 when the churchyard was enlarged by taking in a portion of a field to the east of the building, and presumably the road altered accordingly. This suggests that the original road, the old Fosse Way, may have taken a curve to the left where the present entrance to the newest churchyard is, and wound around closer to the original wayside chapel, to come out on the Littletown Road. There is some site evidence of this, but like all else in this area, there is plenty of work to be done on field investigation.

The mill, still known as Manor Mill, is only a few hundred yards down the road, on the corner of Honiton Bottom Lane. It was in use up to thirty years ago and the present owner hopes to have it working again. There can be little doubt that this was the Domesday mill, another indication being that it was once known as 'Dungeon Mill', which is not as ominous as it sounds, the word dungeon coming from the medieval 'donjon', derived from the Latin dominus or lord, so that a dungeon was just a lord's possession, i.e. the lord of the manor's possession as described in Domesday. Behind Littletown House, which no doubt once formed part of the mill buildings, is a forty-foot well with twenty feet of water.

Nearly every early settlement was located near a good water supply. Littletown had a good source in the Gisseage, which is said to have got its name from the fact of its rising in a hedge on the Gittisham parish boundary - and hence Gitt's hedge, or Gisseage as it became in time. It was natural for the inhabitants to spread out along its course, and in fact within living memory the actual bed of the river formed a roadway from Littletown to the present High Street, known as Watery Way.

It would have been natural for this trackway up the Gisseage then to have turned east along the course of the streams that flowed down from the lakes (which were later channelled on either side of the High Street) towards what appears to have been the established route from Dorchester to Hembury along Northcote Lane. And from thence up what is now New Street to the original settlement at St Michael's, rather than the other way around. The junction with the Hembury route would then have formed a pivotal centre

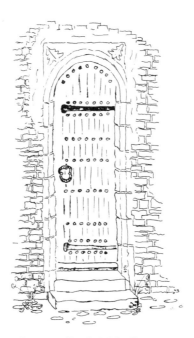

Norman doorway in the south-west wall at St Michael's

St Margaret's with 1807 almshouses cut off by the Exeter road

2

Although Domesday listed sixteen ploughs in use on the Honiton manor the general trend throughout the county was away from arable farming to an intensification of pasture with the growth of the wool industry. It was a trend largely dictated by conditions. The sixteenth century historian William Camden wrote in *Britannia* of Devon that 'the soil is poor and lean .... it is almost quite barren in most parts unless it be overspread with a certain sand from the sea ... and therefore in places more remote from the shore, it is bought dear.' A contemporary of his, Tristram Risdon, agrees in his *Survey of Devon*, adding 'on the east part of the shire the mould standeth most upon white chalk, which is passing good for sheep and corn; a little farther it consists of a red and blue marle, which is not rocky, but an earthy substance; this soil is most natural for pasturing of beasts ...'

The Honiton district seems to have been particularly rich in this marl, defined as a decayed chalky soil much used as a general fertiliser from the Iron Age to the nineteenth century. There were over forty marl pits within a two-mile radius of the town, some within the town itself, hence Marlpits Road and Marlpits Hill today, which might suggest that it could have been an industry in itself and exported to other districts away from the coast where the sea sand was 'bought dear'.

This particular soil appears to have favoured sheep rearing, and Devon, particularly the eastern part, became one of the most important wool-producing areas in the country. The manor of Honiton was recording substantial sales of wool in 1286, with a fulling mill in operation by 1244, and by the end of the fourteenth century the town became the third most important cloth town in Devon.

It is interesting to note that prior to the Norman Conquest the wool fibre was exported to the Continent in a raw state, where it was in great demand.

While there are many allusions to woollen manufacture in England from early times the native industry of the island could not match the products of the Continent and it was William I who recognised this and took steps to rectify it. He brought over Flemish weavers to settle in Carlisle and Edward III followed this up by importing weavers, dyers and fullers to settle throughout the country teaching their art.

11

The wool trade continued to expand in the years that followed, with every encouragement from the government. Edward III had his Chancellor sit upon a sack of wool as a reminder to his Lords that England lived off the backs of its sheep, as tradition still has Chancellors do today. And in 1678 an Act was passed making it illegal to bury the dead in shrouds 'made or mingled with flax, hemp, silk, hair, gold or silver or other than what is made of sheep's wool only ...'.

Early in William III's reign the kersey cloths became less favoured than the mixed worsted serges which proved more profitable. Honiton is believed to have been the first Devon town to make these and by the end of the eighteenth century most of the population for twenty miles around was busy spinning, weaving, dressing and scouring and fulling the serges. Honiton was living very nicely off the backs of the sheep.

Littletown from the railway embankment, 1895

While wool might be called the bread and butter industry, it was in the making of lace that Honiton became, and still is, world famous, although today it is mainly practised as a craft.

How and when the making of pillow lace, that is bone or bobbin lace made on a pillow, was introduced into the region is unclear. As early as the thirteenth century England had excelled in the making of ecclesiastical embroidery, and the art of needlepoint is reputed to have come to this country with the influx of religious refugees from the Continent. However there is no firm evidence to show how the craft of the pillow lace, for which this area became famous, took root here, or why it seems to have been confined to an area bounded by the coast and the rivers Axe and Exe.

But we do know that by the seventeenth century it was a thriving cottage industry, for a tombstone in St Michael's churchyard records that in 1617 one James Rodge was a bonelace seller in Honiton and he was apparently wealthy enough to give £100 to the poor of the town. And in 1630 county historian Thomas Westcote writes of Honiton lace as 'a pretty toy, now greatly in request' and that in the town was 'an abundance of this bone lace.'

By the year 1698, of the 4695 lacemakers in the area, 1341 of them were in Honiton. This fact, allied to Honiton being the principal market town in the area and situated as it was on a main trading route, making it the best collecting point for the lace made in the villages around, led to Honiton providing the generic name by which this particular lace has become so well known.

A rather less wellknown craft associated with the town was the making of pottery. Bernard Leach, the eminent potter, says that 'to dig a single clean clay in the vicinity of the kilns was the habit of the old country potters.' This certainly applies to Honiton, and even today the 30 feet deep seam of clay still lies under the site of the old pottery at the east end of the High Street.

The first potter on record, in 1763, was a Samuel Ford, with a Flood and a Hussey mentioned towards the end of the century. The early product was a coarse red earthenware fashioned purely for everyday use. The potter who raised the craft to an industry over a century later was James Webber who began producing a higher quality type of brown earthenware, including ornamental and decorated pieces, which he took by horse and cart into Exeter to sell in the streets.

By 1881 Webber was doing well enough to move to better premises about fifty yards away which became the location of

Honiton Pottery for the next 110 years. Under his successors the business developed, producing finer quality hand-painted ware. Charles Collard was instrumental in exporting it worldwide, and on his retirement in 1946 it became a limited company, Honiton Art Potteries Ltd, who abandoned the use of the local clay in favour of a more dependable variety from a neighbouring county.

Other trades and industries have flourished in the town at various times. Over the years there have been six flour mills, two breweries, two tanneries and an iron foundry; also a soap factory in Streamers Meadows and a butter factory in Littletown.

The twelfth and thirteenth centuries saw immense changes in Devon, comparable in scale only to the industrial revolution. It was the age of the boom in boroughs newly created by the lords of the manors who conceived that it was more profitable to rent land to tenants than to keep them as feudal servitors, and to raise dues from markets and fairs, and any other privileges they could think of. It was above all a young man's world, when a great deal had to be done in a short time - the average life span was only around thirty years.

Between Domesday and the Black Death (1348) there was a tally of seventy-four boroughs in Devon, sixty-one of which were newly created, more than twice the number for any other county. The peasantry who populated them put up the houses and shops, the workshops, the mills, developed the trade and the emerging industries such as wool and iron. Today thirty-one of these boroughs survive as towns. Honiton is one of these, so that again we can accept that it was a thriving and busy centre long before the records confirm its official recognition at the eight-day parliament in Lincoln in 1300, to which Honiton was invited to send two representative members, Johannes de Swengethull and Galfridus Toleiner.

By this time the ownership of the manor had change hands. The de Mortain family who had gained it in the Conquest had fallen into disgrace and their property was transferred to a new royal favourite, Richard de Redvers, who was also given the old title of Earl of Devon around 1106. The de Redvers family or de Vernon, as they were also known from a family estate in France, have the credit for founding the early market town of Honiton sometime between 1184 and 1212. It was a William de Vernon who came under the favourable attention of King John who seems to have interested himself in the de Redvers family and in Honiton. On a visit to the town in 1201 the King granted a charter for the market to be held.

There was a sequel to this which introduces a very colourful character into Honiton's early history - one Faulkes (or Falco) de Breaute, described at the time as 'a Norman, a bastard of mean extraction' who was nevertheless also a personal favourite of King John on account it is said, of his 'great personal courage and strength'.

In 1216 William de Vernon's son Baldwin died at an early age and his widow Margaret, or Margery, his young son Baldwin and all his estates became, as was the custom, in the gift of the King. King John promptly presented her in marriage to Faulkes de Breaute, who thereby assumed wardship of the young Earl and management of the Honiton estates. That it was done promptly is borne out by the *Testa de Nevil*, the 1235 revision of Domesday, which records that 'Margery, sometime wife of Baldwin ... is in the gift of our lord the King (since the death of her husband 1 September 1216) ... and was married to Falco by King John's assignment ...'. King John himself died on 19 October the same year - roughly six weeks after Baldwin.

The marriage seems to have lasted only a few years. In 1221 the Pipe Rolls of John's successor Henry III refer to Falco de Breaute as 'holding the borough of Huneton by reason of his wardship of Baldwin de Re(d)vers by grant of our Lord the King,' and of his owing 'a palfrey for having a yearly fair at the manor of Huneton on eve day and morrow of All Hallows.' But three years later Falco was dead, poisoned on his way to Rome having been banished by Henry following 'a life of great vice'. The thirteenth century chronicler Matthew of Paris calls him 'that impious, ignoble and base conditioned of men Faulk de Breaute,' and there is no doubt he was something of a medieval adventurer. Whether his marriage to Margaret was romantic or merely expedient is questioned in an enigmatic epitaph which Matthew quotes as 'being written on his marriage', the translation from medieval Latin reading:

Law, love and union bind them together,
But, what kind of law?
What kind of love?
What kind of union?
An unlawful law, an unloving love,
And a disunited union ...

Faulks de Breaute has left a recognisable link with the world today - among the many properties he owned through the king's patronage was a manor in Lambeth where he built a mansion which he called Faulkeshall, and which we now know as Vauxhall.

Over the ages the manor of Honiton seems to have been something of a moveable asset and passed around independently of the family estates. In 1210 William de Vernon (or de Redvers), inheriting the title and estates from his brother Richard, gave Honiton to Richard's widow, Hawise, for life providing she did not impose any extra taxes on the townspeople. It reverted to the main stream on her death, until Isabella de Fortibus, the last of the de Redver family, willed it to Edward I on her death in 1293.

Edward in turn bestowed it 'for good services' on Gilbert de Knovil in 1297. But by 1324 it was back with the family estates, probably through purchase by the Courtenays, who inherited the title and estates on Isabella's death.

The Courtenays were a family of noble French descent. A Richard de Courtenay, having abandoned his French estates, came to England in the entourage of Henry II's wife Elinor. Their connection with Honiton came through the marriage of a Robert de Courtenay to a Mary de Redvers around 1200, resulting in their great-grandson Hugh inheriting the Earldom of Devon and the attendant estates when the male de Redvers line died out.

The founding of the Powderham branch of the family was the result of another favourable union, that of Hugh Courtenay in 1315 to Margaret deBohun, heiress of Powderham Castle, where the family still live today. This marriage was to be the salvation of at least the cadet branch of the Courtenay family, for Hugh, or perhaps his wife, willed the Powderham estates to their sixth son Philip - together with that ubiquitous asset, the manor of Honiton. The main estates and the title were lost for the time being with the extinction of the senior branch of the family through treason, Thomas de Courtenay being beheaded in 1461, possibly through choosing the wrong side in the Wars of the Roses; Henry Courtenay, newly created Earl of Exeter, meeting the same fate in 1538. Henry's only son, Edward, was confined to the Tower, to die in exile in 1556, stripped of all possessions.

The Courtenays of Powderham were left to carry on. A baronetcy was bestowed on William Courtenay in 1644 and a viscountcy on another William in 1762. There was also the offer of the title of baron to yet another William in 1689 as result of his espousal of William III's cause. The Earldom of Devon itself was eventually restored to the family in 1831. It is interesting that, through all, the Courtenays retained the manor of Honiton until the nineteenth century.

There seems to have been a family tendency to sail close to the political wind. In 1402 the inheritor of the Powderham Estate, Philip Courtenay, with sixty of his men, kidnapped Leonard Abbot of Newenham and brought him and two of his monks to the Courtenay house in Honiton, where he kept him confined for fifteen days. Just what was his object, whether hostile or protective, is unclear. The Lollard movement for the reform of the church was at its height, but Newenham, near Axminster, was one of the remotest monasteries and hardly likely to be a target. Moreover the Courtenays were overall a staunch Catholic family. Philip's action incurred the wrath of the King and he was imprisoned in the Tower for a short period for this and for 'other offences.'

There is no doubt that the Courtenay family was a great power in Devon in the Middle Ages, if not the greatest, with a pedigree which few in Europe could equal. They were certainly the largest lay landowners in the county until well into the middle of the fifteenth century, when they fell victim to the York-Lancaster struggle.

3

The origin of the name of Honiton is peculiarly difficult to attribute. Varied and imaginative deductions have been made. It appears in Domesday as Honetone and in later records as Honetona, Hunitone, Hunniton, Hunington, and Honyngton. The 'ton' is one of the most common elements in English place names, meaning stockade or encampment. It is the 'honi' that seems to lack definition. Tentative explanations include 'honey' from the bees that legend says used to swarm in the valley; 'hone' from local whetstone; 'Huna' from one of the early villeins and, most colourful, honi' from the French word meaning shame or disgrace and relating to an ancient fable of the barren ladies of the town who were directed by the priests to spend a day and a night in the chapel of St Margaret's, the patron saint of pregnant women, to remedy this condition. Whether or not it did is not known.

The nineteenth century clergyman and writer, Sabine Baring-Gould, relates the 'hon' to the old Celtic word 'hen' meaning old; and historian P.V. Polwhele believes it to be of Saxon origin and coming from 'onnen y tun' meaning 'town on the river bordered by ash trees.' the 'ey' or 'y' being Old English (OE) for river. There is another possibility that the OE word 'hoh', meaning the smooth rounded end of a hill referred to the prominence on which St Michael's stands and Honiton could mean the town on the rounded hill.

The matter is likely to remain unsolved in the absence of a more definitive explanation. There is also another puzzle connected with the town - the origin of the borough seal, surely one of the oddest in the country. Its original meaning and date is lost in antiquity, but the present form was presented to the borough in 1640 by Sir W.J. Pole, of the prominent local family. The earliest description, in the *Notitia Parlimentaria*, is of a coat of arms depicting 'a priest instructing a demi-child erased, in chief a hand couped, in base a growing plant.' Today it is accepted more or less as a pregnant woman addressing an idol with an obstetric hand above and a flower below.

This attempt to tie in the plight of the supposed barren women of Honiton suggested another explanation from historian W.G. Willis Watson who thinks the contents of a Roman lady's jewel case found in the ruins of Pompeii might shed some light on the matter. Among them was a necklace hung with curious amulets, such as objects in coral which were supposed to promote fecundity, and a closed hand with the two fingers extended to ward off the evil eye. This does seem a likelier guess as to the meaning of the so-called flower and the rather chilling analogy of the 'obstetric hand'. However, here again is a bit of unresolved history.

Town Seal

The first actual mention of Honiton as a town appears to have been in 1178, when it was included in the eight towns on which Richard de Redvers was assessed to the crown 'in the sum of £10.' That it was something of a commercial centre within the next hundred years is illustrated by an incident of the time. At this period Jews in England were restricted to certain towns for trading in order that they could be checked for payment of tallage, and they could only move to other towns by special permission.

However, one Jacob of Norwich chose to come to Honiton without the king's licence to live here, with the result that, according to the Rolls of the Exchequer of the Jews dated 1270 'the Sheriff is commanded that he take into the King's hand all Jacob's goods and chattels and keep them safe ...'. He would have been brought before the Justices of the Jews and possibly returned to Norwich. However it is interesting to note that while Honiton was not one of the towns where the Jews could live and trade, Jacob of Norwich seems to have considered it worth the risk.

The annual fair for which Falko de Breaute owed a palfrey in 1221 continued to be held with various alterations. In 1247 the licence was granted to Guy de Rupe Forti and the day changed from the feast of All Hallows to the feast of St Margaret. Ten years later King Henry granted it to Baldwin de Insula, to be held on the Monday, Tuesday and Wednesday in each Whitsun week. It stayed in this form more or less, the actual date being the Monday after 19 July, until fairly recent times.

The early years of the town were overshadowed by the economic decline which affected the region even before the Black Death struck in the autumn of 1348. This bubonic type plague entered the country at Melcombe Regis, Weymouth and spread with terrible rapidity through the West Country. Before it was over it killed off between one third and one half of the population of England and produced a social, agricultural and administrative revolution that, with the sudden decimation of the working masses, swept away the old feudal system and marked the emergence of a middle class.

19

Devon suffered particularly badly with its population reduced to around that of the eleventh century. But it was also one of the first counties to commence recovery. By the end of the fourteenth century the people were already beginning to regenerate the neglected countryside and within the next century farms were restocked and working profitably again. Building was now becoming a major industry and, of most importance, the cloth trade, on which the regions depended, was back to normal.

The thirteenth century had seen a new kind of taxation levied, the taxation of personal property. But such was the effect of the depression that this had to be drastically cut in the next hundred years, in some cases by as much as 74 per cent. Honiton's reduction was 23 per cent, suggesting the town was not on the poverty line.

Apart from the town itself the whole countryside around had undergone a transformation. Many new farms were established with the consequent diminishing of the woodlands; moorland had been ploughed and names such as Heathpark usually had their origins in the type of land turned to farming.

Information as to local events in these early times is sparse. Two kings, Henry III and Edward I passed through the town in 1230 and 1297. In 1268 a tenement holder called Roger le Stur was hanged in the town for felony, and in 1286 an enquiry was held into the death of Richard de la Hulle, killed while robbing the Dean of Rouen's granary at Ottery St Mary, the French names, it seems, lingering two hundred years after the Conquest.

Honiton's early parliamentary representation was short-lived. In those days the town had to pay salary and expenses of their members of Parliament. After only ten years the two burgesses decided to recall Johannes and Galfridus on the grounds that they could no longer afford their support. The town reverted to government by the Portreeve (from the OE *portgerefe* - officer or governor) who was accountable to the county Sheriff, with a short period as a municipality in James II's reign.

It was not until 1640 that Honiton decided they wanted parliamentary representation again and in this the burgesses were supported by two eminent local men Sir William Pole and Walter Yonge of the Shute area who were the first two members to be returned.

4

The twelfth and thirteenth centuries were also the great age for the building of churches in Devon. While Honiton waited until the nineteenth century to build St Paul's there were four chapels to cater, at various times, to the spiritual needs of the town.

Of these the most important, as it became the parish church, was St Michael's. Of the other three only Allhallows and St Margaret's can be accounted for today. The fourth, a chapel to St Thomas, has vanished without trace. A mention of it is made in Bishop Grandison's Register of 1332 as having been licensed for divine service, and there are references to local bequests up to 1528. But today no one can say with any certainty where it stood or what happened to it.

St Margaret's stands on the outskirts of the town on the Exeter road. And although this busy road now runs right through the complex of buildings and burial grounds connected with the chapel, it was not always so.

Nothing definite is known about St Margaret's original foundation and endowment. The earliest reference is to a forty-day indulgence granted by Bishop Brantyngham in 1374 to all who contributed to its support. But there is an interesting account which ascribes the endowment to a crusading knight named de Tracy, a natural grandson of Henry 1, whose family came from Gloucester but owned land in Awliscombe. This de Tracy is believed to have been the knight of that name who was one of the assassins of Thomas a Becket and who, to expiate his crime, joined the Holy Crusades. During his time in the East he is thought to have suffered from leprosy and to have recovered, and on his return home to have commemorated his recovery by founding St Margaret's and endowing it for the care of four leprous persons.

That he did take part in the assassination of the Archbishop is supported by a confession he allegedly made to the Bishop of Exeter in which he said of the event 'their spirits which had been raised to the highest pitch gave way when the deed was perpetrated and they retired with trembling steps ...'. A branch of the family settled in Honiton and built their house, Traceyhayes, on the slope of St Cyres Hill overlooking the leper colony and chapel, and it was a descendent of theirs, Dr Thomas Charde, last abbot of Forde, who, observing that the building was falling into decay, almost totally rebuilt it.

He completed his work in 1530, so that with his restoration and enlargement the hospital consisted of 'five apartments, one for the governor and four others for four leprous people, with an handsome chappel annexed for God's service'. In the graveyard then surrounding the chapel are reputed to be buried the remains of those executed for their part in the battle of Fenny Bridges in 1549. In 1807 four new almshouses (costing £293.13.6d.) were added, no longer needed for lepers but for the poor and needy of Honiton who each had a separate cottage and garden. Today this group is split up, divided by the comparatively recent line of the Exeter road, and separated into private ownership. The old road, once part of the Fosse Way, running along the north eastern boundary and now known as St Margaret's Lane, was once called Beggars Lane from the tramps and beggars who, on their way to the town workhouse, used to hide their personal possessions in the hedgerows or in rabbit holes, to be retrieved later.

The fourth chapel was Allhallows, situated in the centre of the town. Again the exact date of its origin is unknown but there is a reference to it in the Cartulary of Newenham Abey in connection with a convocation held there in 1327.

It is believed to have been built as a place of worship for wayfarers, which would support the theory of the early road coming down through Northcote Hill along the line of the main street and continuing northwards towards Hembury. This would have put Allhallows on a main route for a number of years even if only as a wayside shrine to begin with. In 1429 the people of Honiton petitioned the Pope to be allowed to use the chapel to celebrate mass on account of the difficulties of climbing the hill to St Michael's in bad weather. This was granted, as was permission for a bell-tower and bells at the town's expense. In due course, as we shall see, it was mainly demolished and became the site of the new parish church of St Paul's.

The lovely old church of St Michael's is now relegated to a sort of secondary parish church. From its early association with the beginnings of the settlement around Littletown it was natural for it to become the parish church, a status retained even when most of its congregation drifted away with the expanding borough.

Work on enlarging the ancient chapel was commenced in 1406 by the lord of the manor, Richard Courtenay, but proceeded slowly after he became Bishop of Norwich in 1413 and after his death two years later it ceased altogether. It was left to another Courtenay Bishop sixty years later to recommence the work. Peter Courtenay's diocese was much closer to home. On his becoming Bishop of Exeter in 1478 he attacked the rebuilding with great vigour and completed the tower, the nave and most likely the south aisle all within a couple of years. In 1483 he donated the oak screen. After his death in 1491 improvements to the church were carried on by wealthy parishioners, notable among whom were Joan and John Takell.

In order that the new parish church of St Paul's might be built in the town, St Michael's was demoted to a chapel of ease in 1835. But we do know that extra land was acquired three years later, in 1838, to enlarge the churchyard, St Michael's still serving the parish in extremis. In 1911 St Michael's was badly damaged by fire.

Although it is now only used periodically it has never been made redundant, and in many ways, even after 150 years of relegation, it still has closer ties with the town than St Paul's. Town space allowed of no burial place beside the new church, so the dead still come here for burial, and many of the living still prefer to be married and christened here. It is still used for periodical services and is still subject to regular diocesan inspection, with the Allhallows Charity contributing to the maintenance of the church fabric.

It has also a special link with a particular section of the community in that it is the traditional burial place for gypsies of the area, and many of those born around Honiton follow the custom of returning, from considerable distances sometimes, to bring their dead for interment here.

Very recently a somewhat new role has been found for St Michael's as periodic display centre for local arts and crafts in connection with town events such as the Honiton Festival.

St Michael's from the south

23

5

The shape of early Honiton can be clearly defined today. The borough boundaries were laid out along what is now the lower part of the main street, with burgage plots allotted to each householder. These are rather more clearly defined on the south side of the street, their southern boundaries precisely determined by what used to be called Hind Street, now King Street. The borough would have extended from roughly just west of the Gisseage, where the Market Cross used to stand, up to the junction with Clapper Lane. Beyond this was known waggishly as Scotland. The borough boundary was not extended until the Reform Bill of 1832.

Although now the entire main street through the town is known as High Street, up to at least the early nineteenth century the lower end was called Fore Street, meaning primary or first, as against the High, or ascending, end. Polwhele, at the end of the eighteenth century describes the town as consisting 'principally of a broad street running from east to west, and another (not so long) from north to south'. The latter would have been New Street and Northgate Lane, the latter considerably wider than it is now, and the former much narrower.

That, more of less, must have been the extent of the early borough. But it is interesting to note that it was not until the eighteenth century that Honiton's main street began to be as linked up with the outside world as it is today. As recently as the second half of the nineteenth century Farquharson wrote 'all the roads, or nearly so, approaching the town are modern.' And he describes that section of the Exeter Road west of Honiton, linking the old Turks Head with the Sidmouth road, as 'a new thoroughfare' cutting through the grounds surrounding St Margaret's. 'It is quite evident' he says 'that the road from Exeter to Honiton on its reaching the Turks Head turned to the North and wound around at the back of the Grange, and also continued on the South past the chapel, thus approaching Honiton by a circuitous route'.

The eastern end of the High Street is of comparatively recent construction too. Up to at least the 1790's all eastbound traffic, including the stagecoaches, curved right up New Street, turning left into what used to be Warwick Lane and is now Queen Street, on up the present Pine Park Road to the Copper Castle on to the Axminster road. The site of the present road entering the town from this point was originally a narrow path called Shipley Lane which joined Hale Lane and then became a footpath across a field known as Shipley Close, coming out opposite Marwood House. In 1795 this track was widened, in connection with the Paving Act of 1790 to take traffic directly into the top end of the main street. On all maps of the period Warwick Lane is indicated as the London road and when one thinks of the number of coaches using this route daily, in addition to the regular traffic, one feels for the coachmen.

The road to Taunton at this time was down Clapper Lane, through Combe Raleigh, Luppitt and Smeathorpe.

New Street today

6

Honiton has been very fortunate in escaping the devastation of war, possibly because it has been very adept in minding its own business, which in turn may have been an art born of necessity. Exeter was noted in early times for the number of sieges it suffered and Honiton, only fifteen miles away on the main London road, must have been in a most advantageous position for the besieging armies to use as a support base. While the city was pre-eminently loyalist, in 1137 it found itself besieged during the civil war between two royal claimants to the throne, Matilda grand-daughter of William the Conqueror and her cousin, Stephen. And on this occasion it was Honiton's lord of the manor, Baldwin de Redvers who held Exeter for Matilda.

Three times subsequently Exeter held out for the king; in 1467 against the Yorkists and in 1497 against Perkin Warbeck. But it was in the third of these sieges, in 1549, that Honiton came closest to being involved in actual warfare.

The battle of Fenny Bridges, which took place only two miles east of the town, is not a famous encounter. In fact few people outside the area have heard of it. Yet it could be said that the success or failure of the Western Rebellion, which has been described as the most formidable opposition to the Reformation which England saw, hung in the balance that day. Fenny Bridges was as far as the rebellious western army got in its march eastward.

The seeds of the uprising were sown in a general national unrest. Henry VIII had been dead for two years and the reformation of the church, which he had begun, was still steam-rollering along, albeit at a slower pace, under his weakly son Edward and the Lord Protector Somerset. Times were hard and the country people particularly were also suffering from the dissolution of the monasteries ten years earlier, with the parcelling off of church lands to uncaring new owners. Many were without work and faced with higher rents, with none of the charitable assistance the monks had offered.

It was a situation in which the church with its old and comforting rituals was of increased importance. Now these were being swept away with the Reform of the Prayer Book, the English form of service and the abolition of many of the old Catholic practices.

While the rest of the country protested in various ways, it was the West Country that rose in full-scale rebellion. The uprising started in

Cornwall and was triggered by the government's deadline of Whit Sunday for the introduction of the new form of service. It rose in a groundswell of angry Cornishmen led by Humphrey Arundell, a young soldier and member of a distinguished West Country family. As they marched east they were joined by hundreds of Devonians. There were skirmishes at Sampford Courtnay and Crediton but no serious opposition. The growing army headed for Exeter.

From the outset this was a passionate declaration from the people, unlike many other regional uprisings where the peasantry were often manipulated by the landowners to serve their own particular cause. This was a spontaneous combustion and had the rebels had more experienced leadership to harness their fury and fierce determination they might well have succeeded.

As it was London appears to have been remarkably apathetic in its response. This peasant revolt seemed a long way away and the Lord Protector, gravely underestimating the situation, contented himself with sending west two old Devonians, the Carews - uncle Sir Gawen and nephew Sir Peter - who had estates in Mohuns Ottery, near Honiton, and who felt themselves fully able to deal with this bit of local trouble. However they soon found things beyond their attempts at diplomacy. Lord Somerset sent another trouble-shooter, Lord John Russell, again armed with little more than sage advice and irrelevant instructions.

Lord Russell made contact with the Carews, and as the Carew family owned a house in Honiton (where the Three Tuns is today) it was apparently decided the town would make the natural base for operations. It was a decision which on this occasion must have presented Honiton, a committedly Catholic community, with some heart searching, and it is not surprising that Lord Russell's efforts to raise some sort of army met with little success, especially as he did not have much money to pay them with.

Meantime the rebels had reached Exeter. Had the city joined them the end result might have been very different. But while many of the workers living there slipped away to unite with them, among those left practical issues won the day. The cathedral clerics, while mainly disapproving of the new services, considered it prudent to support them; the merchants had their commercial interests and the mayor declared for the king. The siege began on 2 July, 1549. With fresh reinforcements of rebels arriving every day, it is estimated there were around ten thousand surrounding the city.

Exeter waited for Lord John Russell to come to their relief. And he was waiting for an army. Reinforcements promised by Lord Somerset failed to arrive. Of a hoped for two thousand foot soldiers raised by the local gentry loyal to the king, only four hundred materialised and these, when both money and back-up failed to arrive, started to drift away.

On 17 July Somerset dispatched a body of mercenaries, some four hundred horse and around eighty foot soldiers, composed of Germans, Italians and Spaniards. Mercenaries were quite commonly employed by governments to fight alongside local forces, until the middle of the seventeenth century when national armies came into being.

But they were not popular with the people and Russell's contingent made slow progress on this account, being 'so odious to our people ... we can hardly move them to receive them without quarrell ...'.

With their arrival Honiton must have assumed the aspect of a busy garrison town with all the trials, and advantages to some, of accommodating these gathering troops. But the fact that they had to be billeted even though they were foreign, incomprehensible, strange mannered and brought in to fight good Devonians, with whom the Honiton people must have secretly sympathised, doubtless made for an explosive situation. It was a situation that had its difficulties for the mercenaries, too. For while fighting was just a job of work to them they did on this occasion apparently resent having to fight people of their own Catholic religion, and many of them had made it a condition of service that they should afterwards to be taken to Rome for absolution.

Lord Russell grew increasingly uneasy, still waiting for more troops under Lord Grey and the Welsh contingent promised with Sir William Herbert. Rumours of uprisings all around, no doubt fuelled by the Honiton innkeepers, stories that Exeter had fallen, that the rebels were marching west, eventually decided him to fall back into Dorset and wait there. But Sir Peter Carew went after him in hot pursuit and persuaded him to return to the town. Again he waited with growing pessimism and shrinking funds.

Just when it seemed that the latter had run out Russell received a surprising deputation in the form of three Exeter merchants who had been caught outside the city when the siege began. They were two ex-mayors, John Perriam and Thomas Prestwood, and a businessman

John Bodleigh (whose son was to found the famous Oxford library). They were all rich men with personal and financial reasons for supporting the king and from their own funds they brought the harassed commander 'such a masse of monye' that he could at least keep the army he had intact.

He was heartened enough to make a few exploratory forays outside the town, after one of which, running into an enemy roadblock, he retired nervously to Ottery St Mary where 'in a fit of pique' he set fire to most of the town before returning to Honiton. But the rebels were meanwhile itching for a fight. And their enthusiasm, fired by Russell's indecision, led Arundell to make a bad mistake. He decided to strike before the new government reinforcements could arrive. Had he waited it now seems very probably that Exeter would have fallen within three or four days and the whole situation would have been vastly altered.

On 28 July Russell received word that the rebels had advanced up the road from Exeter as far as what is now known as Fenny Bridges and then as Feniton or Veniton Bridge, just over two miles away. Apparently hoping to take them by surprise he appears to have taken the northern Hembury road out of Honiton and approached the Exeter road west of Buckerell, through Deer Park. Here he assembled his men and surveyed the rebels gathered in the water meadows below and holding the principal of the several bridges spanning the leats and streams into which the Otter divided at this point.

Lord Russell's attack was led by the Carews at the head of their experienced cavalry. For a time the rebels held firm. Then they were forced to fall back, spreading into the meadows alongside the road. Russell followed up immediately with his foot soldiers who initially suffered severe losses from the rebels' longbows. But in the infighting which followed the bowmen were at a disadvantage. Also the government forces were likely to have been much better equipped, being probably armed with arquebusses, the forerunner of the musket, and possibly some cannon. The rebels may have had a few hand-guns but in the main most likely had to rely on billhooks and pikes and fierce determination.

Eventually Arundell's men were forced to fall back towards Exeter. Then the account has it that the mercenaries, underpaid and undeterred by scruples from exacting what they considered the legitimate spoils of war, went to work stripping the corpses. So busy were they, the story goes, that they failed to notice the arrival of two

29

hundred and fifty brawny Cornishmen until a rain of arrows cut short their grisly work, whereupon they fled in panic before the furious onslaught of the enraged enemy. However new reinforcements were arriving from Honiton to join Russell's force and the tables were again turned. The Cornishmen, greatly outnumbered, had to join the main rebel body retreating to Exeter.

It was the beginning of the end. Lord Grey's forces had arrived and been joined by Spinola with another assorted band of mercenaries. London was at last taking the matter seriously and diverting forces from other parts of the country. Within a few days of the battle Russell left Honiton for the last time and pressed on to Exeter. There were some clashes around the city but the day was won for the government with the battle of Clyst Heath where Arundell's force was badly defeated.

The siege of Exeter was raised on 6 August, 1549, just over a month since it began. Of the rebels who fought and lost the veteran soldier Lord Grey said 'such was the valour and stoutness of these men that .... he never in all the wars he had been in did know the like.' The whole Western Rebellion petered out by the end of August with the rounding up of pockets of resistance in Somerset. Arundell and three other rebel leaders were imprisoned in the Tower and later executed. By one of the ironies of politics the Lord Protector was by then fallen from grace and himself a prisoner.

It was an event that could have been momentous and in fact is almost forgotten. Today there is little to mark the battlefield of Fenny Bridge. As you drive over the bridge on the Exeter road the land to the right, where it was probably fought, is now solid and drained, the leats channelled off. Cottages have been built there and the railway line bisects the area. But if you turn right at the bridge, to Feniton, and go under the railway bridge, there is a level hedged-in field at the right of the road, green and peaceful, which the local people still know as 'Bloody Meadow.'

7

Honiton is not notable for its fine mansions, possibly due to a greater diffusion of land ownership in Devon compared with neighbouring counties. The monied families connected with the town tended to have their seats elsewhere - the Northcotes had their manor at Monkton; the Courtenays, following their inheritance of the de Bohun estates, were based at Powderham; the Younges and the Poles and the Putts all lived at distances outside the town.

The one fine mansion the town possesses, Marwood House, was built by the family of possibly Honiton's most interesting character, Dr Thomas Marwood, in 1619. Fortunately it has escaped being either burned down or turned into an inn and exists today looking, outwardly at least, much as it must have looked then.

Dr Marwood was a Honitonian by adoption, and late adoption at that, for he was around seventy when he decided to settle in the town sometime after 1581. Yet the most remarkable part of his career was only just starting and in the next thirty-six years he went on to achieve medical fame and honour at Court, married two more wives and devoted half a long lifetime to the poor and sick of his adoptive town.

He came of a North Devon family who moved south and he was born in Colyton around 1512. Deciding on medicine as a career he took his degree at Padua in Italy, then the most celebrated medical school in the world.

Tradition has it that he was physician to Elizabeth I although this is not borne out by any evidence and was probably a natural codicil to his having been summoned to London in 1593, at the advanced age of eighty-one, in company with a Mr Fowler, surgeon of Budleigh, to attend the Queen's favourite, the Earl of Essex. Essex was suffering from a 'diseased foot' that the court physicians had not been able to cure. Apparently in those times, when medical knowledge was in its infancy, it was not unknown for some provincial practitioner with a particular line of study to be summoned to London for consultation with the rich and royal.

The choice of Marwood may have come about through his apparent association with the Courtenay family. Some thirty years earlier, before he came to Honiton, he had been entrusted to accompany the ailing Earl, Edward Courtenay, on a journey to his old

31

university at Padua following the latter's release from the Tower and was with him when he died. Thus information of his connection with the famous teaching college may have reached royal circles. Happily it seems the two doctors were able to treat the Earl of Essex's feet successfully and there is mention of him paying a visit to Honiton in April 1596.

Thomas Marwood had already been married and widowed, with four children, before he came to Honiton. When he was eighty-seven he married Christine Serle, herself a widow with four children, whom he outlived to marry yet again, at ninety-four, a lady named Temperance Thatcher in 1606. He died in 1617 at the age of one hundred and five.

Although his fame today centres around this alleged royal appointment, his own passionate concern was for the people of Honiton, the town in which he spent the latter part of his life.

He leaves proof of this in his will. After small bequests to his children and step-children, who had doubtless made their own ways in life and must have been quite elderly themselves when he died, he directs that 'the poor of Honiton' shall receive the 'piece of land called Grubblehayes, with the rents of some other tenements, to be distributed yearly in the church porch'. He also left two other properties to house eight of the poorest in the town, with a trust of money and certain rents from a piece of ground called Bear-parke towards the support of eight poor people (the Marwood Trust is still going today as part of the Honiton United Charities). His tomb, he says, is to lie a little within the porch of St Michael's and to be 'decent and of a convenient height' and for his son John to add to his obituary 'such other phrases as he thinks fit and convenient'. Carved on his tomb, lying today a little within the porch' of the church is 'Here lieth the body of Thomas Marwood, Gent. who practised Physick and Chirurgery, above 75 years, and being zealous of good works, gave certain Houses and bequeathed in his Will to the Poor of Honiton, 10 pounds and being aged above 105 years departed in the Catholic Faith, September ye 18th Anno Domini 1617'. There is no mention of any court status either by his direction or in any other phrases his son thought fit.

Two years afterwards John built Marwood House. It was a pleasant Jacobean mansion that Charles I visited on two occasions in 1644 when he came through Honiton on his way to and from Exeter. This was during the Civil War, and at a time when battles were being waged all over the West country Honiton was again playing host - this time to both sides. As can be imagined it was a situation not without its risks. Prior to the King's visit Prince Maurice had spent some time in the town with his foot soldiers, and in October 1645 Lord Goring led a detachment of royalist troops through at midnight on his way to Blackdown. But the next day Sir Thomas Fairfax marched a main body of parliamentarians in for a night's lodging before going on to Cullompton. There must have been some agitated burgesses during that twenty-four hours.

Marwood House, 1809. The house passed by marriage into the Tucker Branch of the Marwood family in 1764

8

Honiton had become more a place where business was transacted than battles fought. There are instances of important documents and letters patent being dated from the town and, in 1590, when Exeter was in the grip of the plague, the Devon Lent Assizes were adjourned to Honiton.

But while the town as a whole maintained its neutrality its citizens did on occasion take up arms in causes about which they had personal feeling. The Monmouth Rebellion was such an occasion. There was strong feeling for the Duke in the West Country and following his defeat at the battle of Sedgemoor twenty-three people from around Honiton were tried at Exeter in September 1685 for their part in the uprising. Four men - a young surgeon named Samuel Pots, John Oliver, Henry Knight and John Knowles were executed in the town and are reputed to have been buried within the precincts of St Margaret's. Others were sold as slaves to plantation owners abroad. A ghost of these bitter 'Duking Days' is said to haunt Lower Marlpits Hill, that of a fugitive rebel attempting to return to his cottage just above St Michael's church who was waylaid by a party of government troops and summarily hacked to death in front of his wife and children.

This wild, gaunt figure in broad-brimmed hat and flowing coat is alleged to have been seen from time to time, and the most fully recorded account is of a party of schoolchildren walking up the hill with their teacher, near the cottage, in1904, when apparently the figure appeared walking towards them. They were so distressed, and their descriptions so identical, that the headmistress unearthed the story surrounding the cottage and in the 1930's it was pulled down. Its site was visible until quite recently, but there do not appear to have been any more hauntings.

It was during the Great Rebellion of 1688 that Honiton achieved distinction as the scene of bloodless manoeuvres which James II admitted in his memoirs were the turning point in his fortunes.

Whilst the invitation to William and Mary to come and rescue the country from James and Catholicism, and his attempts at royal absolutism, had come from Tory and Whig leaders alike in Whitehall, not all the people were convinced of William being the right choice to replace him. In the West Country particularly there had been doubts.

That they existed in this area is reflected in a most interesting letter written from Utrecht on 8 January in 1688 to Sir William Courtenay from his brother-in-law William Waller, who was at the time in attendance on William and Mary at the Hague.

Part of a letter to Sir William Courtenay from his brother-in-law in Utrecht, 1688.

In it Waller stresses the royal couple's 'zeall for the Protestant interest and the Welfare of poor England'. He roundly condemns the false rumours that have been circulating regarding their sincerity, in particular those stemming not only from the 'inveterate mallice of the French' but also from the 'mallice of England likewise'. He refers to a plot afoot to instigate divorce or separation between them and to 'marry Her Royal Highness elsewhere ...'. He begs Sir William to satisfy their friends on these points and on others which might have caused a weakening in their resolve.

From this it would appear that the doubts about the invitation centred around the couple's sincerity in the Protestant cause, and that the plot hatched with the connivance of Mary's chaplain and contacts in England and 'two of her women who were in the confederacy' to separate them and to ally Mary, the closer claimant to the throne, with another consort was one way out. However William and Mary, as the letter reveals, would appear to have quashed any such efforts and to have committed themselves to 'nothing conducing more to the Wellfare of the Kingdom then uniting and healing the unhappy Divisions in it ...'.

Waller also mentions that he has spoken to Prince William of his writing and that the Prince 'approved and said you would thereby much oblige him'. He goes on 'I have written to severall others I hope with good success,' and asks to be informed 'how this newes is relished'. He urges Sir William to 'endeavour to have it spread as much as may be among both Gentry and Comonalty and favour me with an account of its progress ...'.

Sir William's efforts among the 'Gentry and Comonalty' would appear to have had some success locally. In April of the same year the king's electoral agent in Honiton reported that the corporation 'was composed of country gentlemen perverse to your Majesty,' and billeting arrangements for William's troops in the vicinity of the town were made well in advance of his landing at Torbay on the 5 November. However in the latter area the groundwork does not appear to have been so effective and by the time he and his sizeable body of cosmopolitan troops reached Exeter on the 9 November his reception had been so lukewarm that he apparently began to doubt the whole venture.

Nevertheless the news from Honiton must have been heartening enough for him to send on an advance force under the command of Col. Tollemarche to the town. Here the Colonel and his staff took up quarters in the Dolphin, one of the Courtenay inns, with other officers spread around other inns and a body of troops in the Shambles. Meanwhile things were not going too well with James. Many of his most trusted commanders were deserting, among them Lord Cornbury who was in command of an advance cavalry force at Salisbury. Here, according to one of his officers, Major Ambrose Norton, a plan to defect with a body of troops was put into action. At five o'clock on the morning of 12 November three of the four regiments marched out, led by Lord Cornbury, Sir F. Compton and Lieut-Col. Langston. They made for Axminster, but here the commanders were loyal to the king and Compton was sufficiently influenced by them to take most of his men back to Salisbury. Cornbury and a fellow officer stuck to their resolve and with a small body of men, pressed on to Honiton, followed shortly afterwards by Langston with his corps. Thus the die was cast, for Honiton by now was regarded as rebel territory.

Arriving in the town they were 'received as friends'. The officers were put up in the Dolphin and the men billeted around the town. And in the morning there was a general muster at the Market Cross at eight o'clock for the purpose of giving all defectors a chance to change their minds if they wished. Major Norton, with Lord Metham, two cornets and a quartermaster, plus thirty-four troopers, decided not to desert. The officers were imprisoned in the Dolphin and the men confined in the Shambles.

Although the body of men declaring for William was small by comparison, the psychological effect on the surrounding countryside was dramatic. Catherine Macaulay, the English historian, wrote of it 'the moral effect of this insignificant loss of men was very damaging to the Stewart cause'. William took new heart. From all over the West Country wavering supporters had their minds made up for them and flocked to his cause. News of this spread throughout the country. Defections from the king's ranks were the order of the day. Hugh Speke, a royal spy sent to find out William's strength at Exeter, happily joined forces with the rebels when he got as far as Honiton and 'communicated all' to Colonel Tollemarche before going on to Exeter to join William. At one time it was said that William had more Catholics in his army than did the king.

By the time William advanced to Honiton on 21 November he had a force of around eleven thousand foot, four thousand cavalry plus an assortment of over six hundred sailing vessels following him up the coast. He did not stay long in the town, but pressed onto Axminster where he stayed for several nights. While there he is recorded as having paid one shilling and sixpence 'for a guide and one horse for the Lord Cornbury to go to Honiton'. Possibly to do some settling up in the town, for it seems that while there they did some shopping. A newsletter of 13 November records that while they were in Honiton the Prince of Orange ordered for his troops '7000 pairs of shoes and 7000 yards of cloth ...'.

It must have been a stirring two weeks or so for the people of the town. And probably profitable ones too with every inn full to overflowing. But above and beyond that must have been the pride of knowing that the name of Honiton was known far and wide as the venue of the fateful rendezvous which most likely influenced the future course of English history and helped to make the revolution a virtually bloodless one.

With William's advance the message of 'a free parliament and the Protestant religion' swept the country. The civil population rose to his banner. Not even the Tory belief in the divine right of kings was strong enough to prevent James's chief supporters like John Churchill from deserting him. On the 11 December, less than a month after William's landing, James fled to France. It was a massive defeat on all accounts. One of those with him when the news of Cornbury's defection was announced said then 'it seemed to pull up all his hopes and expectations by the roots...'.

The part played in all this by the Courtenay family, and in particular Sir William Courtenay, is made clear in a letter written by the Earl of Shrewsbury, William's new Secretary of State, to Sir William on 2 April 1689, less than two months after William succeeded to the throne. In it the Earl says that the king 'having thought fitt att this time to confer Titles of Honor upon some persons whom he thinks the most deserving of them that they might bee remembered by posterity to have contributed with him towards the Settling of this Nation' has conferred upon him the rank of Baron of England and asks him to choose the title he wishes to assume.

The Secretary also adds that he does not question 'but it will bee so much the more acceptable to you as that it is owing to the king's immediate favour and his opinion of your deserts'. Which would suggest that the award was not a run-of-the-mill inclusion in an honours list of those who had supported him, but one made by the king personally for an important contribution.

9

In spite of the high toll exacted by plague and other pestilences the population of Devon almost doubled during the next hundred years, both by natural means and by immigration. Exeter was now one of the fastest growing centres in the country and Honiton grew along with it.

In 1700 the famous novelist Daniel Defoe visited the area and was greatly impressed. Honiton, he wrote, appeared 'a large and beautiful market town very populous and well-built'. He particularly liked the streams running beside the main road 'so that every family in the town has a clear, clean running river (as it may be called) just at their own door...'. Although this was hardly an uncommon feature in the West Country where many hilly towns with available springs had the same feature.

With the eighteenth century the town added another industry to its livelihood - hospitality. The roads of Devon were notoriously bad and Honiton, almost halfway between Axminster and Exeter, was a welcome stop both for private travellers and for stage-coaches, then a growing service. Inns and taverns must have sprouted up like mushrooms. At the height of the coaching era there were thirty-five inns open at one time around the centre of Honiton and over the years at least sixty have been counted.

Only five have survived today. One of the great coaching inns the Angel closed its doors comparatively recently, and the picturesque landmark, the Black Lion on the corner of New Street, was demolished in 1967 to widen the access. Of those left the New Dolphin (New because the original was largely destroyed by fire in the eighteenth century) is still central to the town, as in the past it seems to have been the scene of most of Honiton's historic happenings. There is a theory that at one time the original building was the town mansion of the Courtenay family on the strength of the Courtenay crest, a dolphin, being found on one of the old walls and a reference to it in a deed of the sixteenth century as being 'lands of the heirs of William Courtenay'.

Old Honiton looking east

Old Honiton looking west

While the Courtenay family certainly owned the Dolphin, as well as several other properties in the vicinity, they also owned, as part of the manor, the old Golden Lion which was closed as an inn in 1851 and is today in commercial use and still called the Manor House. It is a fine wide-fronted building on the north side of the lower part of the High Street (Fore Street earlier) with a flint elevation under the present plaster coating. It has a nineteenth century porch and an extra storey has been added. It does seem a more credible possibility, from family background, appearance and position in the town, as having been the Courtenay town mansion.

Still with us, too, is the interesting little inn farther up the High Street - the Red Cow, famous as the gypsies' haunt in the last century when one of the great entertainments of Fair time was to go up to the Red Cow for a pint of ale and watch the gypsy men fighting and the gypsy ladies arriving in their velvet and feathers.

Honiton's position on the beaten track to the west has always meant a flow of traffic through the town, by foot, by horse, by coach or now, by car. People are apt to recall it often as the town they 'passed through' on their way somewhere. Diarists, travel writers, all have been this way and most seem to have been complimentary about the town in their perambulations. Charles Dickens, as a young reporter on the Morning Chronicle, stopped at the Golden Lion on his way back from Exeter in 1835 after covering the current General Election. He had ordered a meal and a change of horses for his postchaise when he spied a rival journalist, Denison of The Times who had also been covering the election, pulling in for refreshment. Dickens sped off without his meal but apparently in time to get his story in first, although he did not leave his impression of Honiton.

Quite a few kings and nobles have passed through. Some have stopped. Princess Victoria, four years before she became queen, stopped at the Dolphin for her carriage horses to be changed.

The execrable condition of the roads out in the countryside was nearly as bad in the towns where it was often almost impossible to make a way through the confusion and obstruction of the main streets. Honiton was no exception and may in fact have been considerably worse than some. So that there must have been some misgivings when George III decided to pay an official visit with his family in 1789 on their way from Weymouth to Plymouth. But a way was found to present His Majesty with the town's more acceptable face. The royal

41

party was met at Copper Castle 'by the Portreeve, many inhabitants and 350 young ladies all dressed alike, with white ribbons'. For while the town might be unprepossessing the mothers of the young ladies seem to have done their best to make up for it.

This welcoming party then proceeded to lead their royal guests, not back through Warwick Lane and New Street, the usual route into town described as 'then a slum', but down Shipley Lane, which was a footpath, to Hale Lane then across the field called Shipley Close to come out at the east end of the town - the route which, as already mentioned, became the extension of the Axminster road into town, today known as Kings Road.

George III greeted by the ladies of Honiton

Much of the chaotic condition of the streets must have been largely due to the calamitous fires that plagued the town from the late seventeenth to the beginning of the nineteenth century. There were other fires from time to time but this particular period of expanding population, vastly increased traffic with the attendant anxiety to pack in as many travellers and their horses as possible, late hours breeding carelessness with candle and lantern, seems to have been particularly disastrous, especially when you add the fire hazards of the drinking and rioting of Honiton's wild electioneering period.

Little is known of the first two recorded fires of any severity in 1672 and 1699. But in 1747 there was 'a great conflagration which burnt half the town.' It started in the main street, in a house opposite Allhallows Chapel and 'burnt from thence the whole south side of the street to the bridge at the west end of the town and a portion of the Shambles.'

An even worse outbreak came eighteen years later in 1765. This began in a blacksmith's shop, again on the south side just below the King's Arms, spread across the road to a malthouse and had both sides ablaze very quickly. It burned from noon on the 21 August until 3 o'clock on the 22nd and consumed 115 houses, extending up to the old Presbyterian Chapel. Its intensity melted the bells in Allhallows tower and destroyed much charity property around, also the house in the middle of the street. There is a gruesome story of the Presbyterian chapel schoolmaster, a Mr Darke, going back into his house to fetch some papers and being burned alive. It is said his hand and a piece of his arm were found grasping the latch of the door.

There was a lapse of some years before the next bad fire in 1790, when a blaze broke out in the stables of the Golden Lion. Fortunately the main building was not harmed, but the flames spread rapidly into the street and destroyed 39 cottages. Not long afterwards in 1797 another outbreak just below Clapper Lane accounted for 49 cottages and in 1817 a row of weavers' cottages behind the Dolphin were demolished. The last of the ravaging fires seems to have been in 1840, when the old Swan Inn and several houses were destroyed, the Baptist Chapel being built on the site.

There were those who profited. In an 1830 street directory at least fifteen fire insurance offices are listed in the town, each company having its own fire-fighting service, and if a building was ablaze which did not carry their particular 'fire mark', i.e. a metal plaque affixed to the wall, they would gallop by regardless.

The townspeople themselves did what they could by forming a watch, taking turns to parade the streets at night with tubs and buckets ready and a fire-engine was presented to the town by a successful parliamentary candidate, Lawrence Cox, around 1774.

This constant fire alert was not always appreciated by visitors. A correspondent of the Gentleman's Magazine, writing of Honiton in his 'Gilpin's Tour of the West' had this to say of his visit to the town: 'We intended to stop but it was ordered otherwise. The town having twice been burnt down in the last thirty years ... at about twelve o'clock a fellow began his operations with a monstrous had bell and in a hoarse voice informing us that all is safe. This serenade is completed every quarter of an hour.' The result being, he pointed out, that every visitor to the town was forced to become an unwilling night watchman. His party apparently lost no time in moving on.

Part of a bill for repairing the Dolphin following the fire of 1797

10

Whether it was the king's visit or the townspeople's embarrassment over the state of their town, a few years later, in 1792, the Act 'For Paving and Otherwise Improving the Town of Honiton in the County of Devon' was presented in Parliament and duly approved by His Majesty.

The preamble to the Act paints a sorry picture of the conditions prevailing: 'Whereas the Great Western Road leads though the Town of Honiton, in the County of Devon, and such part of the said Road as lies within the said Town is in general very inconvenient and unsafe for Travellers, and several of the Streets, and other Publick Passages within the said Town, are not properly paved, cleansed or lighted, and are subject to various Incroachments, Annoyances, and Obstructions, and there is not any regular Nightly Watch within the said Town: And whereas it would be of great Benefit and Convenience to Travellers, and to all Persons residing in, and resorting to the said Town, if the Passage through the same was rendered safe and commodious, and if the said Streets and publick Passages were properly paved or otherwise repaired and cleansed and lighted, and all Nuisances, Annoyances, and Incroachments therein removed, and if a regular Watch was established in the Night Time ...'.

The Act itself, a good quarter of which is taken up with the appointing of Commissioners to administer it, besides decreeing the levelling, paving, cleaning and lighting of the streets, the providing of new drains and sewers and the providing of a 'sufficient number of fit and able-bodied men, armed' to be stationed through the streets as Night Watch, also contained a particularly important proviso in view of the spate of fires. It ordained that no house, or part of a house, or other building, was in future to be covered with straw or thatch 'upon pain of forfeiting the sum of five shillings a day for every day such covering shall be suffered to continue'. Nor were any bonfires to be lit within the town nor was anyone allowed to 'wantonly sport with Torches, Fire Brands or burning Candles in the Street thereof, or let off any Guns, Pistols, or Rockets or throw any Squib ...' subject to a penalty of ten shillings per offence, a fairly heavy fine for the time.

The Commissioners were empowered to set up turnpikes and toll houses at any point leading into the town that they thought fit and to collect tolls therefrom. They could also take down the Market Cross and the Shambles 'and any other buildings obstructing the main street'. Also they had charge of the two streams running down the main street which up till then had apparently been under the jurisdiction of the 'Surveyors of the Town Lakes and the Surveyors of the Highway'.

In the determination to tidy up Honiton all trade signs had to be placed flat on the owner's premises, and shutters, porches, sheds, troughs, rails, steps, pipes and spouts protruding from a building were to be removed. Carriages, wagons, carts and drays were not permitted to wait outside a house except for loading and unloading, nor were any building materials, coal, goods, wares or merchandise to remain any longer that it took to store them. There is one interesting exemption in regard to the building materials in cases where building was actually going on, which must have been all over Honiton, in view of the fires.

Some of the clauses suggest a vivid picture of Honiton town life, at least prior to 1792. For instance there was a ten shilling penalty for anyone 'who shall run, drive, draw, carry, or place, on any of the publick footways ... any Wheel, Sledge, Wheelbarrow, Handbarrow, Truck, or other Carriage, or shall roll any Cask, or wilfully ride, drive or lead any Horse, or any other Beast'. It was also forbidden to slaughter or dress any swine or beast, or 'throw at any Cock or Fowl, in the manner called Cock-squaling ... or cause to be baited any Bull'. There were also penalties for making wheels or shoeing horses or mixing mortar on the public ways, also for throwing out ashes on to the streets and for polluting the streams by washing in them or letting their pigs, geese and ducks stray therein.

The bottom line, of course, to this design for a new neat town calculated to meet with the approval of future travellers, was the levying of a tax on the occupants of 'all Houses, Buildings and Lands within the Town and Parish of Honiton,' of a sum 'not exceeding in the Whole in any One Year of Sixpence in the Pound of the Annual Value of such Houses, Buildings and Lands'. A bottom line no doubt as unpopular then as it is today.

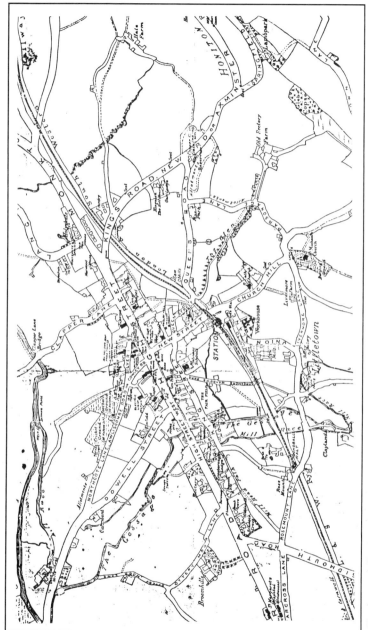

Honiton and district, 1880

It could be said that Honiton is truly the proverbial Phoenix, risen from the ashes of the fires that consumed the town, for all the rebuilding that took place following chanced to coincide with the Golden Age of English architecture, and one doubts very much if the pleasant Georgian and Regency facade of much of the High Street today would exist but for the devastation. Most of the new houses were probably for those who could best afford them and there must have been quite a number of wealthy men in the town at the time. Honiton was still doing very well on the wool industry with employment at a record level. The lace industry, too, was not yet showing any signs of the decline that was to come.

Nor had Honiton forgotten the advantages of playing host to soldiers and during the Napoleonic Wars, between 1794 and 1816, it became a garrison town 'familiar with military life and the pomp of war'. Barracks were built in Littletown, at first for the emergency accommodation of a squadron of cavalry, but by the time the wars ended a Yeomanry Corps, two companies of volunteers, and the HQ of two militia regiments were stationed in the town.

It was during this period that a rudimentary telegraph system was erected on St Cyres Hill, comprising a tall wooden mast with arms raised or depressed like railway signals, which passed on semaphor messages from the one at Woodbury Down.

There was also around this time some move towards provision of better education for the citizens. Previous to the Education Act of 1840 this had been in the hands of charity commissioners, the church, and the grammar schools which were mainly for the sons of the better off. Honiton again was fortunate in the last. It is not known exactly when Allhallows school was founded but it is believed to have been sometime in the seventeenth century. It was housed in part of the old Allhallows chapel and gradually spread to several buildings in the vicinity. When, towards the end of the nineteenth century, the grammar schools generally throughout the country fell into such a deplorable state that the government instituted a parliamentary enquiry, only Crediton and Honiton in the South West appear to have been 'well reported on'.

For the less fortunate of the population there was an effort now to provide some sort of regular teaching. There was a so-called National School in the town as early as 1713, originally in Dowells Lane and later moved to Hind (King) Street around 1829. It was founded for thirty poor boys 'part of them clothed'. The teacher was the church organist. in 1834 the Presbyterian Church was instrumental in opening the British Schoolroom for the education of 'children of the poor in Honiton according to the principles of the British and Foreign Schools' Society' at a cost of £320 plus a parliamentary grant of £150.

There was also a charitable School of Industry in existence in New Street in the first cottage past Summerland towards the station, since demolished. It was run by voluntary subscription to enable poor girls to be taught plain sewing under the supervision of the local ladies, and there is a fascinating little story about the resident mistress there towards the end of the century. She was Nancy Lee, the daughter of a wealthy Cotleigh family. When she was a young girl she had been noted for her beauty and her 'wild ways which eventually led her to run off with the local gypsies and tour the fairs around the country with them. The story has it that during these wanderings she attracted the attention of the Prince of Wales and 'subsequently lived for some time under this protection'. But in the end, her beauty faded and, no doubt suitably penitent, she came home to Honiton where, either through family influence or the compassion of the local ladies she was given the post of resident mistress of the poor girls in the School of Industry. How much she knew about plain sewing must be debatable, but she apparently stayed there until the school closed, when she went to live for a time with a Mrs Loring in a house at the bottom of the town where she kept cats and told fortunes.

Nancy Lee and her cats

There were other Honitonians who carved their names on the wider world in a somewhat different style. There was Ozias Humphry the eighteenth century portrait painter, born in Honiton in 1742, the son of a peruke (wig) maker, who studied in London and came under the wing of Sir Joshua Reynolds and through him received commissions for miniatures and portraits from the Royal Family. He was elected an

Associate of the Royal Academy in 1779 and an R.A. in 1791. In 1792 he achieved the distinction of being appointed portrait painter to George III. He died in London in 1810.

Then there was Captain George Blagdon Westcott, the son of a Honiton baker, born in1753, who joined the Navy as a cabin boy, saw action in the Napoleonic Wards and was made a Captain in 1790. There is an interesting footnote to his story. Following his death at the battle of the Nile in 1798 it is said that Nelson himself called to see his mother in Honiton, on his way to join the Fleet at Plymouth. Hearing that she had not received her son's service medal he took a medal from his own chest and presented her with it saying, or so it is reported, that he hoped 'it is of no less value because I have worn it'.

Another young man of the town anxious to see action was William Guard, son of a Honiton lace merchant, who was born in1773. He chose the army and was gazetted to the 45th Foot in 1789. Stationed in the West Indies he rose to be a Lieut-Col. within ten years. A biographer has rather unkindly attributed his swift promotion to the deadly climate. However, he saw action in other theatres of war, including the Peninsula Campaign under Sir Arthur Wellesley after which he became Lieut-General and eventually Governor of Kinsale. He died in Exeter in 1830.

There was another artist of distinction, William Salter, born in Honiton in 1804 the son of the local town crier. He also went to London to study art and became a protege of James Northcote, R.A.. He also studied on the Continent and is remembered chiefly for his mammoth work, the Waterloo Banquet, which took five years to complete. He had an abiding affection for his home town and painted an altar-piece for the newly-built St Paul's Church in 1838. He became a member of the Society of British Artists and died in London 1875.

It is striking that these young men all seemed to make their mark at around the same time and that they all came from modest families, sons of a peruke maker, a baker, a lace merchant, a town crier.

There is one other name that deserves a mention although she never achieved anything more spectacular than marrying a young man from Blandford in Dorset in 1603. She was Princilla Serle, daughter of an ancient Honiton family, and the man she married was Thomas Pitt. Thus eventually she became the great-great-grandmother of England's famous Prime Minister, William Pitt, 1st Earl of Chatham.

11

With the restoration of Honiton as a parliamentary borough in 1640 there began a period which was to culminate nearly two hundred years later in the name of the town becoming a byword for political skulduggery and corruption throughout the country.

It began as the accepted power game enjoyed by most wealthy county families, in this case the Courtenays as lords of the manor of Honiton, the Yonges of Colyton as big landowners, and the Poles of Shute representing court interests. It was a high profile rivalry fuelled by every variety of manipulation and intimidation, from the 'rotten borough' system of supporting boroughs so small as to make parliamentary representation farcical, to the outright control of 'pocket boroughs', and it did little good for the people it was supposed to represent.

While most boroughs resigned themselves to this state of affairs Honiton appears to have been somewhat more recalcitrant in its attitude. In 1684 these 'alehouse-haunters and poor beggarly rogues' as one candidate contemptuously described them, petitioned parliament for Incorporation and won approval from James II. A mayor, recorder, thirteen aldermen and ten assistants were nominated and became the strong voting force in the borough. In fact it is alleged that only the corporation were allowed to vote and this is substantiated in the 1685 returns which show only twenty-five citizens with electoral rights. However this did not last long. Following the town's 'perverse attitude' towards the King in 1688 and their support for William of Orange, a purge was ordered, throwing the town into 'great disorder and distraction' and within a few months the charter was withdrawn.

Originally the right of election under the Tories was vested in those freemen of the borough paying rates, or scot and lot' (from Old Norse 'skot' meaning contribution and 'lot' being the amount allotted) these inhabitant householders numbering on average between three and four hundred. But in 1724, with the Whigs coming into power, a number of Honitonians not paying skot and lot petitioned the Commons for an equal right to vote with their wealthier neighbours.

To the understandable disgust of the ratepayers the House decided in their favour, ruling that 'every inhabitant in the borough who had a family and boiled a pot there' had a right to vote equal with the rest of the inhabitants 'whether they paid or did not pay scot and lot'. Thus the advent of the 'potwallers' or 'potwallopers'. Where the name first started is obscure, but it is likely of ancient origin and derived from the ME 'wallopen' to boil, so that one who boiled a pot was a potwalloper. When it was shortened to potwaller, this may have influenced the introduction of the obligatory wall, rather than the other way round. It was a franchise not limited to Honiton but also enjoyed by, as far as is known, Westminster, Preston, Southwark, Tiverton, Taunton and Tregony.

Although it might have appeared commendably democratic it was soon wide open to corruption. While the scot and lot citizens earned their right to vote by payment of taxes, the potwallers had no such obligations. They just had to have a household and a pot. The actual wording of the bill did apparently state firmly that the pot had to be 'boiled against the wall in a tenement of their own which had a

Potwallopers

52

separate entrance from the main street which was not enjoyed in common with any other person'. But, with their votes selling for the equivalent of three months' wages, Honitonians soon got around that little technicality. A typical instance of how is cited by historian Farquharson, who relates that his great-uncle, who owned a workshop in what used to be Warwick Lane (now Queen Street), prior to the 1796 election 'had eleven doorways knocked through the front wall and on the opposite wall of each had a small number of fireplaces and chimneys built, and across the floor he had as many lines drawn and he then let these divisions to tenants who entered and boiled their pots and so became free and independent electors for the borough of Honiton'.

Under these conditions voters proliferated until Honiton became known as having one of the biggest suffrages in the country. By 1754 the numbers of voters had risen to seven hundred at a time when there were only twenty-two boroughs with over one thousand.

At the same time according to Hellings' History of Parliament it earned the reputation of being 'one of the most venal boroughs in the kingdom' with an electorate described as 'poor, unruly and of low social standing'. It is pointed out that the poll book of 1763 'does not list a single esquire, few professional men and mostly labourers, artisans and small shopkeepers'.

And they were hell-bent on reaping this golden harvest which had suddenly materialised. If they did not like the candidates on offer they did not hesitate to advertise for others more to their taste. Third candidates were actively sought. It became an open market place for opposing parties, the Tories anxious to put up candidates who would counter this 'democratic faction' and the dissenters importing men like George Shum from one of the Jacobin clubs who furnished him 'with more money than either of his opponents'.

Money was the ruling factor. When George Chambers, son of the royal architect, entered the lists believing all he needed was the backing of the Courtenays and the Yonges, he was soon disabused and forced to go back to London and return 'with £3000 in his pocket' believed to have been supplied by the Treasury. Voters banded themselves into groups in order to get better terms and the key men in the town were the local election agents who acted as brokers. These agents were mostly lawyers and bankers, and chief among them were Christopher Flood and his law partner Mules, the Gidley family, and Townsend and Pearse. Flood had a particular influence with the

THE GHOST OF A ROTTEN BOROUGH

Appearing on the Hustings of Covent Garden

Pd. May 17, 1817 by Tho. Tegg No. 111 Cheapside

54

potwallers through his father, a cobbler in New Street, known as 'Kester, king of the potwallers'.

It is reported that sixteen firms of lawyers fed on the scandal and corruption in the town, with a secondary industry flourishing in the production of political broadsheets and popular verse. During the elections the polls stayed open for a week at a time, the inns and taverns were open twenty-four hours a day with candidates handing out free drinks by the gallon. The whole town was taken over, hustings erected in the main street and members chaired up from the old Market Cross, with meetings held in every available venue.

Defoe, who a few years earlier had been so charmed with Honiton, was, in his later constituency reports, registering disapproval of the 'terrible election mob' there. Namier in his Structure of Politics in 1761 refers to Honiton as being one of the three most corrupt boroughs in England. Lord Cochrane, the celebrated admiral who successfully contested the borough in 1806 and later stood for Westminster, admitted to the House in arguing his case for parliamentary reform in 1817, that he had bribed his way into Parliament for Honiton 'where votes were open, avowedly and unblushingly sold' by paying as much as ten guineas apiece for them. He also, after welshing on a Honiton town treat and incurring debts to his agent which ended in his house being seized, told his new constituency that "a Member who sat for it (Honiton) felt like a man in a dirty shirt ...". And William Cobbett, who had opposed him, agreed to the extent of claiming that Honiton lived by its votes and that representing the town was a practice he could not afford.

Nevertheless there were always the local families who continued to 'afford' Honiton even after the going got rough. The Pole family had represented the borough on and off up to around 1678. But even this early they became disenchanted with the honour and in 1733 Sir William Pole stipulated unequivocally in his will that his request 'to my son John and other persons to whom I have limited my manors, etc., is that they will never stand as a Candidate or if chosen will never by prevailed upon to serve in Parliament for the Borough of Honiton'.

The Yonge family, however, were not so prescient and suffered accordingly. From 1640 to 1768 six Yonges were returned for Honiton, and from 1714 to 1754 Sir William Yonge held many offices under the Crown, was made a Privy Councillor and a Knight of the Bath. Along the way he had become an adept tactician and Lord Harvey's description of him could fit many a good party man today. He was, said the Lord Privy Seal 'good-natured, and good humoured, never offensive in company, nobody's friend, nobody's enemy. He had no wit in private conversation, but was remarkably quick in taking hints to harangue upon in Parliament; he had a knack of words there that was surprising, considering how little use they were to him anywhere else. He had a great command of what is called parliamentary language and a talent of talking eloquently without meaning, and expiating agreeably upon nothing, beyond any man, I believe, that ever had the gift of speech ...'.

In the end Honiton, with its rapacious demands, brought it all to naught. By 1802 the Yonges as a family were ruined. Sir George Yonge, the fifth baronet and last of the family to represent the town, said of the quarter of a million pounds they had amassed by inheritance, marriage and prudence that 'Honiton has devoured the lot'. Nor were the constituents in the least remorseful. When he attempted to stand for the last time without the usual money to bribe them they spat in his face when he came canvassing and one old lady in New Street set fire to his wig with her candle. He was re-elected on his appointment as Master of the Mint but never resumed his seat. The family estates were sold and Sir George secured an appointment as Governor of the Cape of Good Hope, but was recalled under a cloud. He died in 1812 in a grace-and-favour apartment in Hampton Court Palace.

The end of Honiton's political spree began in 1832 with the passing of the Reform Bill. Although the borough held on to its electoral status for another thirty-six years it was finally disenfranchised in 1868. The buying and selling of votes and all the corruption that went with it had been virtually stamped out by 1867 with the second Reform Act lowering property qualifications. This spelled the end of the potwallers. Thus deprived of their income those in dire straits were cared for by the party for which they had voted. The last potwaller was a mason called Charles Ham. Honiton became merged into the county and with the passing of the Redistribution Act of 1885 became the centre of a division. However, even as this goes to press it appears likely that this status will be lost with the merging of Honiton and Tiverton in a new county constituency alignment.

12

The golden harvest had been ephemeral. It left a bleak winter. The easy electoral money disappeared as quickly as it had been gained and the majority of those who had profited by it were mainly those who had lost their homes and shops in the fires - homes and shops replaced by the grander dwellings of the wealthy merchants. But the wealthy merchants were also feeling the pinch of the coming recession.

The prosperity the town had been enjoying from the wool trade began to decline from the middle of the eighteenth century, although its effect was not noticeable immediately because of the many diverse sources of secondary income. One cause of this was the continual wars on the Continent, but more especially it was the competition from the Norwich manufacturers who were producing a much finer fabric than the local kerseys and were able to sell it cheaper. Most European buyers preferred the Norwich stuffs and although Devon merchants tried to emulate them their attempts failed and they were obliged to stay with the coarser druggets and durays which they could sell to the East India Company and to the home markets.

The eventual death-blow was the competiton from the steam-powered Yorkshire mills run on cheap coal and, almost simultaneously, the introduction of inexpensive cotton goods. By 1822 Honiton's wool trade was virtually wiped out, with only one sergemaker left in the town.

The lace industry, too, was in dire trouble. The time of the French Revolution saw a slump in the demand for laces, with a growing preference for simple muslins and gauzes. But again the real decline came with the introduction of machine-made net around 1810, one of the largest of these factories being at Tiverton where some fifteen hundred workers were employed. From around some two and a half thousand lace workers in the town in 1780, the number had fallen to about three hundred by 1820.

All this coincided with other factors contributing to an economic depression. The great coaching days were coming to an end. In 1795 there was a report of fares going up 'due to the cost of fodder'. By 1850 the trains were beginning to steal the traffic, and although Honiton did later profit by them, gone for now was most of the tavern and service trade the roads had brought, together with the buzzing life infused by the coming and going of the coaches.

At this time, too, Honiton said goodbye to the soldiers and the 'pomp of war' and the source of income it brought. With the coming of peace to Europe after Napoleon's defeat the troops were pulled out of the town and the barracks demolished. Although other troops came later, with other wars, and new barracks were built around a century later, their going left a gap in the life of the town.

The culmination, and the 'greatest blow the trade of Honiton ever received', came in 1847 with the collapse of Flood and Lott's Honiton Bank. This could be said to have been the last reckoning of the potwaller era and it cost the town dear. Christopher Flood was a lawyer and, as mentioned, son of the leader of the Honiton potwallers. In 1810 he took in as a partner a Philip Mules and for nearly forty years the principal activity of the law firm appears to have been in the field of local politics, acting as agents and brokers during the vote boom.

Not content with his law practice Flood went into banking in 1795 with a Samuel Lott, son of a Honiton barber, who owned a thriving printing and stationery business and was also local postmaster. There was also another partner named Lathy who pulled out early.

Mainly due to Lott being 'a shrewd man of business' the Honiton Bank, as they called it, had flourished, and appears to have been used by Flood and Mules to support their electioneering operations in securing the return of their candidates, very large overdrafts being involved for the buying of votes. Of the whole concern it was said that 'between their law and their bank they carried things with a high hand', owning large properties and generally wielding considerable power.

This state of affairs seems to have continued happily until around the time of the Reform Bill and Lott's death a year later in 1833. The loss of the shrewd businessman was followed by Flood's death ten years later in 1843 at the age of eighty-four. By this time things were in a state of disintegration. Their respective sons had taken over. Christopher Flood (Jnr) who became the first reinstated mayor of Honiton, is described as 'a most amiable, easy-going man who prided himself on his horses', while 'Harry Buckland Lott spent large sums adorning his mansion and grounds at Tracyhayes'. They took little interest, apparently, in the bank which was left in the hands of two clerks.

The actual collapse, when it came in 1847, is blamed on the demand for payment of a large sum in cash, which the bank was unable to meet, by the National Provincial Bank. However this, while it no doubt triggered the run on the bank, could hardly have been the fundamental cause. This must have had its roots not only in the general economic malaise of the time but to a large extent to the involvement of the bank by Flood and Mules in their electioneering activities. After Flood senior's death the law firm in the person of the surviving partner Philip Mules still owed the bank an 'enormous sum' in this connection, as a result of which Mules had later to leave the country.

Following the National Provincial's demand there is a strange tale of a messenger being sent to Exeter to raise the cash, of his not returning by a stated time and a letter to this effect being sent to the N & P, only to have the messenger turn up shortly afterwards complete with cash 'in gold bullion' and of frantic attempts being made to retrieve the letter. But 'this was not effected'. Perhaps it made the debacle seem a bit less disgraceful, although prior to this there had already been angry depositors storming the bank with their notes and asking for gold instead. That same evening there was a meeting in Flood's house on Zion Hill where 'it was resolved to suspend payment the next day', and the bank was closed for trading.

Two days later there was a general meeting of the creditors of the bank at the Dolphin at which it was revealed that the bank's current liabilities were £91 000 and its assets, including the partners' personal estates, amounted to £180 000. However a further meeting on 16 November disclosed much higher liabilities, in the region of £125 000. Eventually a dividend of five shillings in the pound was paid. Flood was replaced as mayor by J.H. Townsend.

Another banking enterprise, the East Devon Bank, had been set up in the town in 1807 by another three Honiton men, of whom James Townsend also practised law and was also a local election agent. These partners, Smith, Brook and Townsend, lasted fifteen years and foundered in 1822 with a settlement of only sixpence in the pound. However the most noteworthy thing about their venture today is that during their term they became the owners of the manor of Honiton.

This came about with the decision, in 1804, of Lord Courtenay to put the manor up for auction as a result of his having to leave the country to avoid prosecution. The manor and the borough were offered as one lot by a firm of London solicitors, the auction being held at the Dolphin on the 16 October, and comprised roughly about fourteen hundred acres, property in the town including the Dolphin and the Golden Lion, with income from tolls of markets and fairs, and rentals, bringing in altogether around £2740 a year. There was also the perpetual advowson of the Rectory of Honiton valued at £400 per year. The sale details also point out that the borough has the privilege of sending two members to Parliament and the lord of the manor the exclusive nomination of the returning officer. The manor is described as 'nearly coextensive with the Parish'.

In the event it apparently did not sell, for it was again advertised for sale the following March 'in one or more Lots' and eventually, whether by default or purchase, came into the hands of the East Devon Bank.

From the bank the manor passed to Ebenezer Fuller Maitland then to Arthur Champernowne. Somewhere along the line the negotiations became involved in a Chancery suit with the result that after seven hundred years of passing back and forth between kings and earls, the manor of Honiton found itself for a long time in the hands of the Official Receiver. Since then it has been owned by several families. A Honiton M.P. Joseph Locke possessed it for some time and his widow is said to have sold it for £110 000 on his death in 1863, suggesting it must have still retained a good possessory value at that time.

It was bought by another Honiton M.P., the banker Frederic Goldsmid, who sold it to his son Julian. It later belonged to the Beaumont family, who sold it to the Putts, from whom the Marker family of Gittisham bought it in 1880. It is still in the Marker family. The present lord of the manor is Richard Marker who came from Canada in the early 1970s to claim his Gittisham estates on the death of his father's cousin. The manor of Honiton is today no more than a name - the lord of the manor no more than a title. But a title with a long and colourful history.

Lace making

13

Following the collapse of the bank Honiton was left 'in a desolate state'. It affected all walks of life in the town. Tradesmen either went bankrupt or compounded with their creditors. Professional men were hardly better off, and unemployment was consequently at a high level.

Other enterprises met with a similar fate. Two newpapers were started - the Honiton and Ottery Weekly News in 1878, which lasted for twelve issues, and the Honiton and Ottery Gazette and East Devon Advertiser, which did somewhat better and survived a year from November 1883 to November 1884.

Recalling the days when thirty coaches passed regularly through the town, when Honiton was a hub of trade, travellers, politicians and soldiers, contemporary historian Farquharson laments 'but times are changed; the troops are disbanded, the barracks pulled down, the coaches have long since ceased to run. The grass grows green on the roads once beaten bare by the horses' hoofs and the borough is disenfranchised ...'. A dismal picture indeed. But he adds 'Still Honiton flourishes and long may she do so ...'.

So, in a more subdued way, Honiton did. After the frenetic excitement of the election days Honiton people seem to have entered gratefully into the Victorian era. And it is to Farquharson that we are particularly indebted for his first-hand picture of life in the town in the latter half of the nineteenth century when it was making its slow recovery. Money might have been in short supply but the Honitonians still knew how to enjoy themselves, albeit in a quieter fashion than in days gone by.

'Dinner parties were rare', he comments 'and balls rarer'. Teas and suppers were the usual entertainment 'with cards between and spirit and water'. Card games seem to have been very popular, particularly a form of whist called 'swabbers'. Anything in the nature of a big celebration was confined to national events. Among the improvements to the town contributed by the Paving Act Commissioners was the building in 1820 of the Pannier Market next to the Dolphin. It cost around £2000 and the ground floor was designed for the sale of local produce brought in by the country people every Saturday.

The upper storey was the new Assembly Room, a grand hall in which these national celebrations could be accommodated in style, occasions such as the dinner given in 1856 to celebrate the end of the Crimean War, with a big ball the following night. This of course was for the more prosperous, the poor enjoying a dinner on tables spread in the street, with a thank-you tea for the women in the evening.

At this time an agricultural worker's wage was only about eleven shillings a week, out of which he had to pay a shilling a week to the farmer for his cottage and four and sixpence for wheat, leaving only five and sixpence to keep what was usually a large family.

Tallow candles, and rushlights (rushes dipped in fat) for the very poor, were used for lighting. The first sitting room fires of the winter were not lit until the 5 November, and were discontinued after the 1 May 'regardless of the weather'.

Despite the ruling of the Paving Act the 5 November saw fires lighted not only in the houses but in the streets, too. Bonfire Night was not to be without the traditional bonfires, fireworks 'principally hand rockets' and tar barrels set alight and kicked around the town.

At Easter is was the custom to discontinue work by candlelight and the workers made sure this was observed. 'Be the Easter high or low', they sang 'Out the candles we must blow'. On Easter Sunday there was the ceremony of 'clipping the churches', with all the children from the charity schools visiting every church in the neighbourhood and encircling them, hands joined, until the circle was complete and the church 'clipped'.

There was a liking for sport in the town. Up to 1822 a pack of harriers was kept in Clapper Lane by James Townsend, the banker, with several others in the surrounding country until the middle of the century. There were also annual races on St Cyres Hill.

Public entertainments consisted of strolling players and visiting circuses principally. Most years the former stayed for several months performing in barns and skittle alleys, and in 1847 there is record of a troupe of mountebanks playing in a field at the back of the old Kings Arms.

And there was of course always the annual Honiton Fair dating back to Falco de Breaute's day. Originally it was held on the Monday, Tuesday and Wednesday of Whitsun week but this was later made the first Wednesday after the 19 July, with the proclamation by the Town Crier the previous day, a ceremony which still takes place today although there is no Fair to follow any more. The Town Crier still stands in the middle of the town, in his traditional dress, holding a flower-decked pole topped with a stuffed glove representing the symbol of royal permission to found a town or establish a market. He still announces in triplicate 'The Glove is Up. The Fair is begun. No man shall be arrested until the Glove is taken down'. The last promise used to relate to debtors in the town and Honiton police have not found anyone nowadays pressing the point too literally.

Farquharson foresaw the time when this highlight of Honiton's year would be no more. He writes 'the day may not be far distant when Honiton fair will have become a thing of the past ...'. And in order to preserve it 'as I knew it' he has left a detailed description for future generations. Here it is verbatim:

On the Monday in the fair week the country folks used to bring in vegetables which were exposed at New Street corner for sale. On the Tuesday at noon the glove was hoisted and the fair legally commenced. The glove is then carried and placed outside the Kings Arms where it remains (that spot being the centre of the cattle fair held on the Wednesday) till Wednesday night when it is taken to the White Lion for the horse fair held on the Thursday at that end of the town.

During the afternoon (Tuesday) booths and shows would arrive and having taken up their ground would erect their standings. The favourite position for a show was outside the Kings Arms Inn facing down the street. The shows, runrounds and swings always stood east of the Kings Arms. Some years, however, any very large exhibitions would stand facing up street opposite the Baptists Chapel.'

On Wednesday morning the fair would begin in earnest; from opposite St Paul's to Marwood House the horned cattle stood so thickly as to occupy all the roadway. From opposite the Baptist Chapel to the bridge would be pens for pigs and sheep. The centre of the town would be occupied by stalls covered with gingerbread and toys. If there were any Cheap-Jacks they stood opposite the church, and in its immediate neighbourhood were stalls of fancy articles. At noon all the cattle, sheep and pigs would leave the town, but at every road leading out were placed men with long staves to demand a ticket from the drover as an assurance that he or his master had paid the fair 'dues'. The after part of Wednesday was devoted to enjoyment. Every tradesman kept open house where his country customers ate and drank ad. lib.. In the evening the street would be thronged with pleasureseekers.

On Thursday the first part of the day would be quiet but in the afternoon the horse fair would be held at the west end, no horses being allowed higher than the Golden Lion. The stock usually for sale were fit for farm purposes. On Friday the fair being over all the shops were closed and, till late years, pony racing, climbing the pole and even badger baiting were carried on in the street. On Saturday there was a kind of wind-up, some of the shows and booths still remaining and the tradesmen still leaving their customers to see them. During the fair the servants were decked in their best and wore especially smart caps. Of late years the tradesmen have taken their assistants for an excursion on the Friday. Honiton Fair, falling as it does between the hay and the corn harvest affords the farmer leisure time to attend it.

It is interesting that, in this detailed account, Farquharson makes no mention of the hot-penny throwing following the Town Crier's declaration which is a big feature of the present day ceremony. It would seem to be a later addition and possibly borrowed, being quite a common practice in West Country towns at election times when the Regency bucks are said to have delighted in watching hot pennies, or originally hot chestnuts, thrown from frying pans from the windows of inns to the peasants in the street below who scrambled and fought and burned themselves out of genuine need for this manna.

Today the practice (with cooler pennies) goes down well in Honiton and is a great attraction for tourists. Around £100 is thrown into the street every year, subscribed by the landlords, and although there have been occasions when the scramble has resulted in a general punch-up and some people suffering nasty injuries from flying pennies, not to mention the teenage peasants who recently threw the pennies back and broke a window in the White Lion, no doubt it will probably continue as long as the council cares to foot the bill for the necessary public liability insurance.

Honiton still has its street markets every Tuesday and Saturday. The cattle markets have been moved to buildings erected on the north side of the town, where sales are held on Tuesdays.

The maintenance of law and order in the town from earliest times was in the hands of the Portreeve. One old 'Clink' or lock-up was in New Street. There was another, whether earlier or later, in Dowells Lane and back in 1600 it appears from old deeds that one of the county Bridewells was on the site of the old Globe.

There were also town stocks situated near Allhallows which are mentioned by visitors in 1760. These were in use until 1812 when the last occupant was a Charles Ford, 'a great vagabond'. Another deterrent was the ducking-stool, its last recorded use being to duck an unnamed woman found drunk in the cellar of a Mr Gibbon, Maltster, on a Sunday morning. A more common punishment seems to have been to whip offenders through the streets at a cart's tail, the last of these being John Rice and Robert Hill, 'caught stealing apples'. All of which must have provided some entertainment for the public.

But there were occasions when matters really got out of hand, particularly at elections times. In 1763 there is record of a pitched battle in the High Street over a proposal by one of the candidates to put a tax on cider, when the fighting was so fierce that 'the Gisseage ran with blood'.

In 1856 a Borough Police Act was passed obliging all boroughs to have a regular police force of their own to replace the rather haphazard law enforcement that had existed. In its timing it had a double advantage in that recruitment for it absorbed many agricultural labourers then out of work.

The Reform Bill also brought changes in the administration of care for the poor. The Poor Law Act of 1601 had made each parish responsible for those of its inhabitants in need. By the mid-eighteenth century parish workhouses had been introduced, where those accepting parish relief were housed and required to work for their keep either outside of within the institution. Honiton parish workhouse was built in 1738 on land belonging to the Allhallows charity, now Summerland in New Street.

However the need for relief increased on such a massive scale throughout the country, due to the economic decline and to conditions in the wake of the Napoleonic wars, that the parishes could no longer foot the bill and with the Parliamentary Reform of 1832 a new system was devised.

The parishes, while still rated for their own poor, were obliged to join district Unions, under an elected Board of Guardians, which were to establish Union Workhouses and refuse any relief outside them. This meant Honiton building a new workhouse to replace the inadequate premises in Summerland - the Union, on Marlpits Road, converted and extended now to house Honiton Hospital.

It is interesting to note that these parish Unions later formed the basis for local government reform in 1894, when their rural areas became 'Rural Districts' and the town 'Urban Districts' until the later changes of 1974.

Houses on Church Hill Road

14

The decision to build St Paul's church came with the reluctance of a softer generation of worshippers to continue climbing up the hill to St Michael's for services. The offer of a gift of land for the purpose in Hind (King) Street was made by a Charles Tucker of Coryton Park, but this was declined in favour of the site then occupied by the Allhallows Chapel of Ease.

By 1710 the medieval chapel had fallen into a sad state of disrepair which grew so bad that within two years the nave and the tower had to be pulled down before they fell down and a new end was built on to the remaining severed chancel. For thirty years the rest of the old chapel remained a ruin until, in 1743, work commenced on reconstruction which was still unfinished when the great fire of 1765 damaged it extensively. Work was resumed, however, and the new chapel was opened in 1769. In 1790 it was enlarged. In 1835 it was pulled down to make way for the new St Paul's parish church.

The architect chosen for the project was Devon-born, London trained Charles Fowler. Fowler's previous experience had been more in the field of utilitarian rather than ecclesiastical design and he was selected, it is said, for his admirable work on the Exeter Markets. The builder was a local man, William Lee.

Due to the shape of the site it was necessary to position the church north and south instead of the traditional east and west. The stone for the walls was dug in a field at the top of the town 'a little east of Springfield' and the sand used in the mortar came from the same site. The cost of the actual building was about £7600, with the cost of the site and the demolition of the old Allhallows chapel and the clearing of its remains together with those of the charity houses destroyed in the fire adding another £2400. The old bells of the chapel which the fire had melted were recast and hung in the new belfry. The whole amount is said to have been raised by the parish and by the sale of pews.

However, although the completed building in 1847 must have appeared to the Honiton people an impressive monument both to God and to the town's growth, it was beset with structural problems from the outset. Probably the worst of these was Fowler's decision to repeat the innovative use of iron in his market design and in this case to

St Michael's Church today

St Paul's Church today

68

experiment with it for the church roof. Of this Prof. Donaldson wrote in the Sessional Papers of the Royal Institute of British Architects in1868: 'Recollecting the glories of vaulted cathedrals Mr. Fowler determined to cover the nave of Honiton with a ceiling and roof in one which should give him height, be of fire-resisting construction and be of a material that should as far as possible bid defiance of weather and decay. The means at his disposal did not admit of stone so he threw a series of ribs of cast iron across with spandrel ribs at the ends dividing the intervals between each into panels filled in with tiles and cement. In point of construction nothing could be sounder ..'

However, Prof. Donaldson continues. 'one condition was unforeseen, the action of temperature on the mass. The very density of the materials of the roofing rendered cold by the outer atmosphere condensed the hot vapours arising from many hundreds of the congregation produced streams of wet ...'. An Exeter architect,Mr. Ashworth reports that 'great obloquy and ridicule were showered on Mr Fowler the architect for this roof, and he had to defend a law suit and pay heavy damages for the failure of his experiment'.

The roof had to be entirely replaced in 1848 by another firm of builders, Carver and Giles, and the opportunity was taken to add the clock, made by a local craftsmen, a Matthew Murch, together with the chimes. These incidentally were supposed to play 'Britons Strike Home' during the week, and 'The Old Hundredth' on Sundays, a nice Victorian touch. But, as Farquharson notes 'it would be a very acute ear that would recognise these tunes'. They are no longer heard, perhaps just as well.

Seen from a distance the neo-Norman style Fowler chose has an ethereal, lofty elegance which, closer to, seems rather out of proportion to its surroundings. Niklaus Pevsner in his Buildings of England, is guarded in his assessment. He calls St Paul's 'well-built and competently designed'. He finds the tower 'surprising' and while he commends the whole as a 'robust, neo-Norman basilica', he describes it as 'designed as preaching space with galleries'. And he regrets that its 'fine, monumental interior was unfortunately rearranged and subdivided'.

This recent work on the church was in part the culmination of years of patching and mending. Changes had been made. There was a major reseating plan carried out by Edward Warren in 1904. The high pulpit in the centre of the church disappeared and there were other alterations. But in 1985 the point was reached when the fabric was in such a bad state that the building was considered unsafe.

69

Such was its condition that it was actually debated whether or not to close it as a place of worship and sell it off, and reinstate St Michael's as parish church. It was a bitterly fought argument and still echoes. The case for retaining St Paul's was decided on the obtaining of a grant from English Heritage which made it possible for the restoration and alteration work to proceed. The results of that have divided local opinion ever since, possibly as much as the original conception must have divided the town in 1835.

As for the chancel of the original medieval chapel which had survived the demolition of the main part of the building in 1712, it is with us today. It has served as a schoolroom and then, in 1893, as a dining-room for Allhallows School. After the Boer Way it reverted for a time to its original purpose and became, in 1903, a memorial chapel dedicated to Allhallows pupils who fell in the war. When the school was moved from the town in 1938 a use was found for the chapel as a First Aid station during the last war. Since 1946 it has housed the town's Allhallows Museum.

St Michael's lychgate

15

The greatest boost to the Town's economic recovery undoubtedly came from the South Western Railway Company's decision to extend their line from Yeovil through Axminster on to Honiton and Exeter. The Honiton station was opened in the summer of 1860 and the town once again enjoyed the influx of visitors which the decline of the stage-coaches had almost dried up. If the stage-coach had heralded the age of tourism, the railway and, close on its heels, the motor car, developed it into an industry from which the town has greatly profited ever since. New inns opened, local industries revived and the lace making took on a new lease of life with the interest of the visitors.

The town itself was spreading physically. The main street now ran uninterrupted from the Turks Head to the junction with the Axminster Road. The Midstreet houses were gone. The Shambles finally disappeared in 1823. Whereas Dowell Lane was widened with the removal of a house on the corner, the entrance to Northcote Lane had shrunk with the building of a large house on its east corner, an encroachment for which the lord of the manor used to receive a yearly rent. The lower end of Fore Street Hill, so steep that 'the water in the town lake was conveyed down its sides in a series of little pipes one over the other' was raised with the building of a new bridge over the Gisseage in 1807, made necessary when a bad storm caried the weiring down from Littletown and smashed the existing wooden structure.

Perhaps the most striking change was in New Street, heretofore, above its junction with Warwick Lane, a quiet track leading out into the country. But now, with Warwick Lane no longer the main route to London and settled into a quiet life as Queen Street, the building of the railway had transformed New Street into a busy town thoroughfare. New houses, new shops appeared and where the Brookhill stream had crossed the road near the station and under Brookhill Bridge (or Bruckle Bridge as it was called) it was now conveyed under a good road, and solid Victorian houses started climbing Church Hill. There were two private schools and cottages had been replaced by pleasant Regency villas.

With the removal of the workhouse to Marlpits Road Summerland was made over to residential use by the Allhallows

Mrs Fowler's lace shop. Honiton High Street c. 1900

Bottom of New Street in 1953 showing the old Black Lion (courtesy L.A. Collins)

72

charity and above Summerland College a terrace of elegant villas was built. At the bottom of Summerland, across the street, a row of old cottages destroyed by fire in 1887 was replaced by the redbrick terrace known originally as 'Railway Cottages'. Most fortunately the old thatched farmhouse adjoining them survived as Honiton's only remaining Tudor dwelling. Now, of course, the whole surrounding area which, until quite recently was open farmland, has disappeared under housing estates and car parks.

Gas lighting, with the erection of the Gas Works in 1835, came to Honiton on a Friday evening, 23 May of that year.

Although Honiton lost its franchise as a borough with the Reform Act, it was once again incorporated as a municipal borough in 1847, with a mayor, six aldermen and eighteen councillors representing the wards of St Paul's and St Michael's. Then, as now, the town had no official Town Hall to accommodate these new dignitaries.

Reputedly there had been one on the corner of Silver Street which was burned down in the eighteenth century fires, accounting for the corner being known as Hall's Corner, although it seems rather more likely that the name arose from the ownership of property there by a family named Hall in the seventeenth century.

It was therefore apparently decided to build one in 1860 to match this municipal expansion, and a new Town Hall was erected, according to Farquharson's contemporary account, on the north side of Fore Street Hill on part of the site of the Carpenter's Arms and adjoining houses which had been burned down in 1852. The builder was Mr Lee of Honiton. This Town Hall was 'for the dispatch of business both county and borough' and behind it were built police station and cells. That it operated as such is confirmed by White's Gazeteer of 1878-9 which refers to the petty sessions for the Honiton division being 'held at the Town Hall'.

Just what happened to this Town Hall no one seems to know. Or even its precise location. However a consensus of opinion appears to place it on the site of the present police station. When this was built, since the last war, it replaced a much older police station on the same site, housed in a large Victorian building. It seems possible therefore that the old Town Hall of 1860 may have become encompassed in the police station originally at its rear and its purpose forgotten as time went by.

The first clerk to the new County Court here was a Honiton attorney, R.A. Aberdein, and it is recorded that when the coat of arms

High Street, Honiton, c. 1860, looking west

The High Street today, looking west

which used to hang in the old Allhallows Chapel came into his possession he gave it to the County Court to be placed over the Judge's chair. There is no trace of it today in the new magistrates' court nor anywhere else as far as can be ascertained. Like the Town Hall it seems to have disappeared without trace.

Having apparently mislaid two town halls it seems a pity Honiton does not try, try and try again. There is certainly more than ever a need for one in a town of its size.

In1884 the Pine Park estate to the east of the town was sold at auction by James Hussey and a part of this was donated to the town by H.H. Lilley in1935 and forms the pleasant, tucked-away little park know as the Glen, just behind Church Hill. A further addition to the town's leisure activities were the golf links up on the Northleigh Road, formed in 1896 under the aegis of Viscount Sidmouth.

A familiar echo of the past came with the construction of a large military camp on the west end of the town on the south side of the Exeter Road. Heathfield Camp was completed in 1940 and again the town played host to the soldiers. Known today as Heathpark, an industrial estate covers the site.

Education has come along way, too, from the days of the old British Schoolroom. Today we have Honiton Community College and two primary schools plus private and special schools, besides considerable sporting facilities. Regrettably, through lack of space for expansion, Allhallows School was moved to a large old mansion owned by the biscuit family of Peek, at Rousdon near Lyme Regis.

Another loss to the town in more recent times has been that of the Honiton Pottery. Although new premises had been built on the old site after the last war, the business had latterly outgrown them. Attempts were made to relocate it in the town without success. Eventually in 1991 the manufacturing part of the company was sold to Dartmouth Pottery who had the spare capacity to handle the increasing trade and who are still producing Honiton Pottery under its own name. The old pottery in the High Street was demolished, but the pottery shop nearby still carries on as a retail outlet and also as a craft centre where making Honiton pottery can still be practised by those interested in the art.

In the centre of town the widening of the bottom of New Street has undoubtedly helped the flow of traffic into the High Street, but regrettably also meant the sacrifice of the old Black Lion Inn.

The most important latter-day development to Honiton following the linking of the mainstreet with the A30 and its attendant traffic problems has of course been the building of the by-pass in 1966. While it might have robbed the town of some passing tourists it has certainly helped to preserve the fabric of the eighteenth and nineteenth century buildings in the town centre, not to mention the peace and quiet of the inhabitants.

Roofscape from King Street